The
Speak Logic Project

We Promote Better Communication

Application Modeling Tutorial Communication Domain Math

www.speaklogic.org

Download Software
www.slpsoft.com

Contact

To make it easier for us to communicate to each other, the following contact information are given. They can be used to contact us.

Contact Information	Email Addresses
Syntax Correction	syntax@speaklogic.org
Question about Translation	translation@speaklogic.org
All other Information	info@speaklogic.org

Table of Contents

The communication element entity	
The ECF entity	
The separation line entity	
The time line entity	
The progress bar entity	
The error in communication gives rise entity	
The wok entity	
The communicate to arrow entity	
The time and date entities	
The sub function entity	
The note entity	
The node entity	
The callout entity	
The node information table entity	
The communication holder entity	
The external communication holder entity	
The empty container entity	
The reference entity	
The question entity	
The answer entity	
The information label entity	
The point to label entity	
The give rise label entity	
The relationship label entity	
The by label entity	
The dependency label entity	
The agreement label entity	
The match label entity	
The inclusion label entity	
The curl braces entities	
The relationship entity	
Change of communication table entity	
Change of communication graph entity	
The graph line and graph point entity	
The continuity entity	

Group of people entity	
The sub application entity	
The part of application entity	
The sub application result entity	
The sub communication result entity	
The part of application result entity	
The part of communication result entity	
Group part of communication function	
Example Section	

Application Modeling

Introduction

We connect together trough a communication interface that enables us to exchange information. With that communication interface, we can define communication itself as the process of exchanging information. During a communication process, we can exchange information to each other. For example, during an oral communication between me and you, I can repeat a sentence to you; you can also repeat a sentence to me. Whenever we use the term communication here, it means all forms of communication.

Since communication is the only interface that connects us together, everything that we do depends on communication. For instance, we communicate to do our works. With the importance of our communication interface, it is very important for one to understand each other during a communication process. Given that we communicate to satisfy our needs, without the understanding of our communication, our needs would not be satisfied. It is always good to present our communication to the simplest form it can be, so it can be understood. We have already known that any error that is developed during the communication process will cause problems in our applications without being corrected. For that reason, it is always good to analyze our communications and correct errors to prevent problems in our applications.

To better understand the process of communication related to what we do, it is always good to separate the communication itself from its purpose. What do mean by that? We mean that it is always good to separate the communication and the purpose of the communication, which is the application. By doing so, we can have a better picture of the application and analyze it during the communication process and correct any error that is presented before its execution. Utilizing that process allows us to correct errors in our communication and provide us with an error free application. In order to do that, the communication itself has to be treated as a separate entity and then analyzed. Given that what we do includes two steps, the communication step and the application execution itself, during the communication step, we can analyze the communication and make all necessary corrections. In order to have a better view of the communication related to the application, it is always good to have a picture of the overall process. In communication, it is always good to draw the process of the application related to communication to enable us to understand it better. In other words, when we communicate it is always good to draw a picture of what we have in mind or what we intend to do to enable us to understand it better.

To provide us with a better picture of our application related to our communication, it is always good to use diagrams to draw them, so we can analyze the overall process. The Speak Logic Application Modeling enables us to draw the process of our applications related to our communications so we can have a better view of our project. By having a picture of our application related to our communication, we can analyze our communication and correct any error that is presented to prevent problems in our application. There are two ways to look at the usage of the Speak Logic Application Model diagram. We can use it to model what we do, which is our application. We can also use it to model our organizations. For instance if the function of an organization is to develop a product or provide a service, then the project modeling diagram can be used for that; at the same time, it can also be used to show how that organization organized.

This user manual will provide us with some instructions about using The Speak Logic Application Modeling diagram. Given that the diagram is not application specific, the aim of this ~~tutorial~~ is not to connect the entities for us, but to provide us with information about each entity, so we can connect them together depends on our applications. Although the Speak Logic Project Modeling provides us with the simplicity to analyze our applications, however it does not carry any weight at all in terms of error analysis and removal. In other words, error analysis and correction from our applications depend on our communication, not on the Speak Logic Project Modeling. The usage of the Speak Logic Project Modeling assumes the principle of communication is understood. While we can use the modeling diagram to visualize or represent a visual aspect of our application on a computer screen, however the diagram can also be used without the usage of a computer. For instance, we can use the modeling diagram on paper or on a drawing board to represent a visual aspect of our application.

It is also important to note that as well, each entity is considered an actual entity of the underlined entity name. In other words, each entity is considered to be the actual representation of the entity name. We use the word entity in this manual to refer to any entity. Whenever we use the word entity with another name to denote an entity, it represents an actual entity of that name. For instance, we can refer to the communication entity as the actual communication. Whenever we use the word entity here, it means things that exist in life in both physical and non physical forms. For instance an entity can be physical, as well as another entity can be non physical. It is the same as saying that, physical things and non physical things. Here the term non physical entity may also refer to entities that may not be visible to everybody. In other words, those entities exist, but some of us may not be aware of them. In this case, some of us think that they don't exist at all. Thus, those entities are not visible to everybody or identified by everybody.

Understanding the Communication Domain

Given that we communicate relatively about entities that we identify; given that the entities that we identify make our communications possible, it makes sense for us to model our application or what we do accordingly to those entities. Since during our application we communicate relatively or accordingly to the function that we are going to execute, it makes sense for us to model that function accordingly to our communication. The communication domain model enables us to do just that. It enables us to model our application according to our communication. The communication domain model enables us to view or portrait our application according to our communication. In other words, the communication domain model enables us to view our application or what we do, as a function of our communication. Here our communication means the communication of the people who are working in the project.

Since our communication ability is one of our aspects; since communication is one of our aspects, in term of what we do, we communicate in order for us to execute our application. In the communication domain, we model our application related to our communication. In other words, in the communication domain, our application or what we do becomes a function of our communication. For instance, if a function of an organization is to provide a service or manufacture a product, then in the communication domain, this function is being viewed as a function of communication. In other words, the service provided by that organization or the product that is manufactured by that organization, is being viewed as a function of communication of the people who work in that organization. It is very important for us to understand the communication domain. The communication domain model enables us to view or model what we do or our function or our application related to our communication.

Understanding Communication

Before we continue, let's look at some important factor of communication. Keep in mind that based on our understanding, there are three signals entities in communication. We understand miscommunication, in other words, we understand when a communication is unsatisfactory in term of it's contain and its application, we use the red signal entity to denote that understanding. That means we use the red signal entity to denote a communication with error. We understand when a communication is satisfactory, based on it's contain and its application. In other words, based on contain of the communication and its function we understand when it is good. We use the green signal entity to denote that understanding. We also understand feedback, in other words, we understand a type of communication that is related to correction or enabled us to make adjustment to what we do. We use the blue signal entity to denote that understanding.

To better understand communication, let's define it as follow. We have already defined communication as the process of sending and receiving information among us. Now, let's define communication relatively to the way we have defined it. Let's define information as signals, and communication as the process of sending and receiving signals among us. In other words, when we communicate we simply send and receive signals to each other. We do have a sense that enables us to interpret those signals; which is the same as saying that we do have sense that enables us to understand the information that we exchange to each other. To better understand the overall communication process among us, let's look at the diagram below. The diagram below shows that we interface together through communication. We can also say that there is a communication interface between us; for instance "I" and "You" interface through communication.

Communication Interface

I   You

To show the flow of communication, we can replace the communication interface shown above with words that we use in communication. We can also say that rather than using the communication interface phrase on the above diagram, we can simply replace it by interaction elements or by communication interaction element. The diagram below shows just that; we simply replace the phrase communication interface with *communicate with*. In this case, the interface shows that *I communicate with you*. We interact to each other through communication. Whenever we use the term interaction elements, it means that communication elements that we use to interact to each other. For example words, phrases, videos, pictures etc. can be viewed as interaction elements. For oral and written communications, words, phrases, drawings, diagrams etc. can also be viewed as interaction elements.

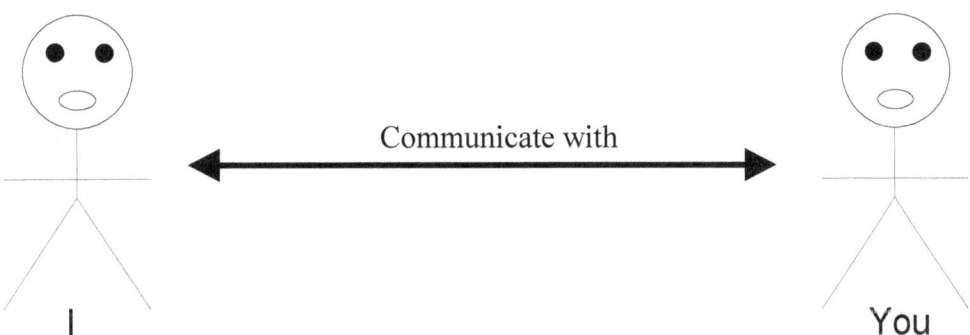

Communicate with

I   You

As we have defined earlier, communication is the process of sending and receiving signals to each other. To better understand the overall process in terms of flow and diagramming; let's look at the diagram below. It shows that I communicate with you, which is the same as I send a signal to you.

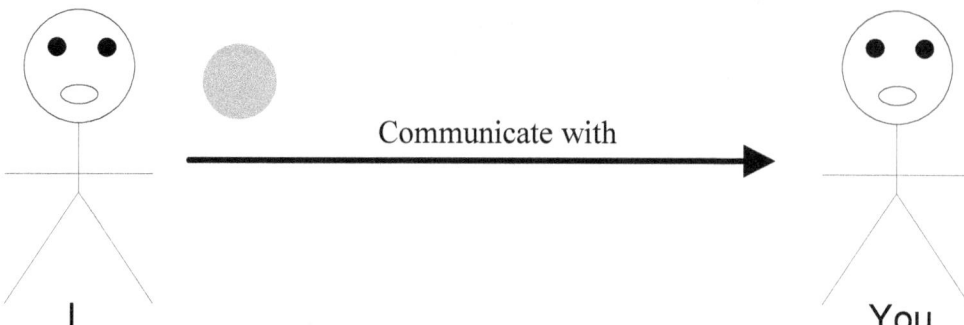

Given that we do have a sense that enables us to understand or interpret the receiving signals, the diagram below shows that after you receive the signal that I send you, then you send a signal back to me. From the diagram above to the one below, it shows that I send you a signal, which is the same as I communicate with you; while the one below shows that you send me a signal which is the same as you communicate with me.

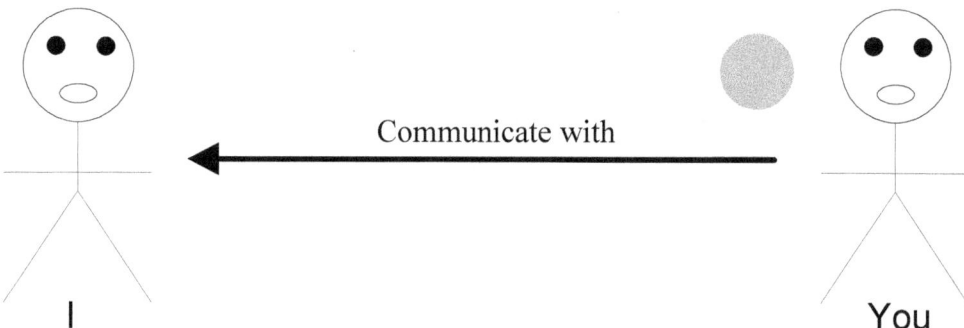

From what we have said above, the overall communication interface which is viewed as the process of sending and receiving signals can be viewed as the diagram below. The diagram below is simply a representation of the two diagrams above. It shows a two ways communication between me and you, where I send signals to you and you send signals to me. In other words, I communicate with you and you communicate with me.

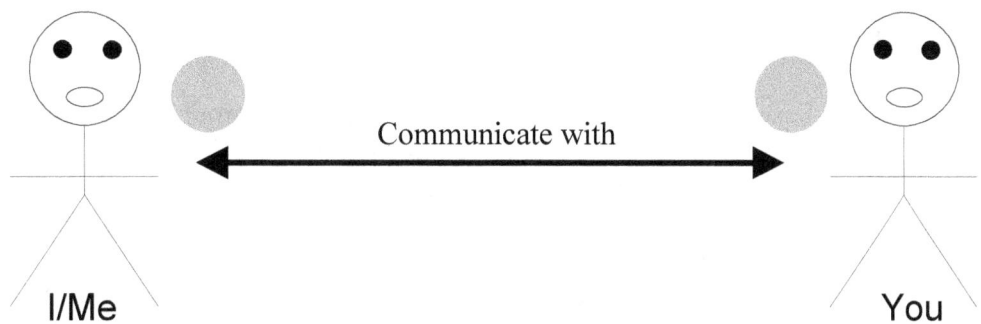

Communicate with

I/Me

You

Application Modeling Entity Identification

As we said earlier, we interact to each other through communication and communication enables us to exchange information. We define information that we exchange to each other communication elements, which are considered as signals. The Speak Logic Application Modeling diagram defines three types of signals. Those three types of signals can be considered as tokens. We use the word token here to denote the dots. We could have also used the word dot. As shown below, the three types of signals are the green token, the red token, and the blue token. Each of those signals has a purpose. The table below gives more information about each signal. To better understand the other entities related to the signals, it is good to take it like that; the signals flow inside and outside to the other entities.

Signals Type	Explanation
⬤	The green signal entity or the green token signal denotes a communication without error; for example, an input sentence without error
⬤	The red signal entity or the red token signal denotes a communication with error; for example an input sentence with error
⬤	The blue signal entity or the blue token signal denotes feedback or parent feedback; this signal acts as a compensator to correct errors; for example, if an input sentence contains errors, this signal will remove the errors and compensate for the removal to make sure the output sentence is error free

The Communication Interface Entity

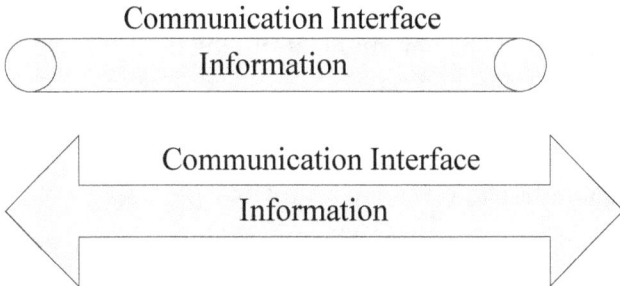

Usage and Description

The communication interface path above shows our communication interface with information included. Since information is what flow through our communication interface, this diagram can be used to show the transmission of information inside our communication interface. In other words, this entity can be used to show that our communication interface carries information.

Available Option

Available options for the communication interface entity include
- Communication interface
- Communication interface path
- Communication interface entity
- Communication link
- Etc.

The Communication Link Entity

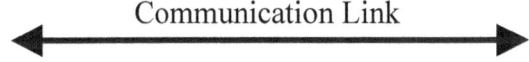

Usage and Description

The communication link entity is the same as the communication interface entity shown above. Communication link is simply another name for communication interface. The communication link is used to show signals path. For example, in a two way communication between me and you, the communication interface shows the direction of the signals between me and you and between you and me. The communication link entity is used to show the directions of our communications.

Available Option
Available options for the communication link path include
- Communication interface
- Communication link
- Communication link entity
- Communication link path
- Communication path
- Etc.

The Left Signal and Right Signal Entity

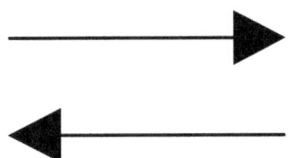

Usage and Description
The left signal entity and the right signal entity show the direction of the signals flow or the flow of the communication. For example, if I communicate with you, which is the same as I send a signal to you, the right signal entity can be used to show that. The same as if you communicate with me, which is the same as you send a signal to me, the left signal entity can be used to show the flow of that communication.

Available Option
Available options for the left signal and the right signal entity
- Left/right arrow
- Left/right signals
- Left/right signals path
- Left signal entity

- Right signal entity
- Left communication flow
- Right communication flow
- Etc.

The Person Entity

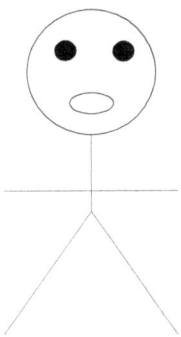 

Usage and Description

The person entity above is used to send communication signals. For example, I communicate with you, this entity represents me. You send a signal to me, this entity represents you. The framed version of the person entity above enables us to connect it with other entities easily. For more information about connecting the entities, see the example section. This entity can be connected with other entities to show the communication of the person. For example, I use communication to solve this problem. In this case, this person entity can be connected with the communication entity.

Available Option

All available options for the person entity include
- I, Me, You, We, He/She, Him/Her
- Person Name
- Person Title etc.
- Person
- Person entity
- Human entity

- People
- Human
- Etc. Includes, employee, employee name, employee with number or employee number, customer, inspector, person with number, tester etc.
- P with index like P_1, P_2, P_3, P_N where N is number of people

The Communication Entity

Communication

Usage and Description

The communication entity is used to show the presence of communication from what we do and the separation of communication from our application. For instance, we can use the communication entity to show communication as a separate entity from our application. The communication entity can be connected to other entities that are related. For example, the communication entity can be connected to the person entity. It can also be connected to the application entity. For example, we use communication to solve this problem. In this case, the communication entity can be connected to the application entity, which is solving problem. The communication entity accepts both input and output signals. It also accepts feedback signal as well. The table below shows the output of the communication entity related to input signal and feedback.

Input	Feedback	Output
Red	None	Red
Green	None	Green
Red	Blue	Green

Available Option

The followings are considered available options for the communication entity. Those options can be replaced by anything that is related.

- Sentence
- Any communication entity
- Any communication
- Communication Entity
- Communication
- Paragraph
- Words
- Etc.

The Word Entity

Word

Usage and Description

The word entity is used to identify a word in our communication. This entity has the same option as the communication entity. As the description says, the word entity can be used to identify a word. For example, the word entity can be used to identify a word in a sentence. The word entity can take both input and feedback. For example, sentence analysis can be done in a word to determine if the usage of that word is understood. In this case, the word entity can be used with the sentence analysis entity, where the sentence analysis entity is used as feedback for the word entity. When that happens, the output of the word entity can be determined by the feedback and the input; see the table below for output result related to input and feedback for the word entity.

Available Option

Available options for the word entity include
- Word
- Sentence
- Paragraph
- Etc.

Input	Feedback	Output

Red	None	Red
Green	None	Green
Red	Blue	Green

The Sentence and Paragraph Entities

Sentence

Paragraph

Usage and Description
The sentence and the paragraph entities are similar to the word entity. The sentence entity is used to identify a sentence in our communication, while the paragraph entity is used to identify a paragraph in our communication. These two entities have the same options as the word entity. For more information about using the sentence entity and the paragraph entity, refer to the word entity.

Available Option
Available options for the sentence and paragraph entities include
- Word
- Sentence
- Paragraph
- Etc

The Communication Function Entity

Communication Function

$f(\ )$

$f(x)$

Usage and Description

The communication function entity is considered to be the function of the communication. It is also considered to be the purpose of the communication. We can also call it application function or application execution function. To the right above is just another way of representing the communication function entity. The communication function takes both input and output. We can say that the communication function takes two inputs and one output. Given that our application includes two instances, the communication, and the application itself. The communication function is considered to be a mixture of the communication and the application in this case. For example, if we talk about fixing a car, then fixing a car is considered to be the communication function. We can also say fixing a car is the purpose of the communication. The communication function takes both the communication and the application as inputs. In this case, to some instances we can say that it takes the communication and the picture of the application as inputs. For instance, if we talk about fixing a car, the picture of the application which is the car is considered as the application and what we talk about is considered as the communication. We can also say the car itself is considered to be the application, while what we talk about is considered to be the communication.

Available Option
Available options for the communication function entity include
- Communication function
- Application execution function
- Application function
- Communication purpose
- Communication Reason
- Project Function
- Function of our Project
- Function of what we do
- $f(\ )$ short name for communication function without variable, any variable can be used to denote the communication
- $f(x)$ short name for communication function with variable; here the variable x is being viewed as the communication
- Etc.

Input	Output
Green	Green
Red	Red

The Principles Entity

Principles

Parent Principles

Usage and Description

The principles entity is considered to be feedbacks that feed other entities. In this case, we can say the principles entity provides feedbacks to other entities that can accept feedbacks. The principles entity provides parent's feedbacks to other entities by sending a blue signal to entities that accept feedback. The table below shows the output of the other entities when the principles entity provides feedback to them. The principles entity only provide a feedback signal to another entity, when the input of that entity is negative or red; see the table below for output result related to the input of the other entity. The way to look at it, the principles entity always makes sure the output of the entity it is attached to is positive. When it is connected preceding an application, we can say that the principles entity is used to make sure that application is always positive or execute without error.

Input	Feedback	Output
Green	None	Green
Red	Blue	Green

Available Option

Available options for the principles entity include

- Principles
- Principle

- Principle of Operation
- Parent principles
- Parent
- Principle Entity
- Parent Principle
- Sentence Analysis
- Error Correction
- Error Analysis
- Analysis
- Error Correction Function (ECF)
- Etc.

The Application Entity

| Application |

| A |

Usage and Description

The application entity represents a picture of our application. Depend how we look at it; we can say that the application entity represents the execution of our application. For instance, if we segment our application into two parts, and we say one part is the communication and the other part is the application process. In this case, we can say that our application includes communication and the application itself. If we segment the same application into several parts, where we also include the communication function entity, then we can say that the application entity is a picture of our application. We can also say a picture of the application in our mind.

The usage of the application entity includes two ways, as we described above. If we segment our application into two processes, the communication process and the application process by itself, in this case the application will depend on the communication. With that, the communication entity connects to the application entity. From that, we have the table below that shows the output of the application based on the communication entity. Again, it is always depend how we look at it. If we use the application entity to show the separation of communication from our application, we can use the application entity as the application execution. However, if we use the application entity to show the step of our application from start to finish, in this case we can say the application entity is simply a picture we have about our application in our mind. Refer to the example section for more information about using the application entity.

Input	Feedback	Output
Green	None	Green
Red	Blue	Green
Red	None	Red

If we segment our application into different sections where we include the communication process or the mixture of communication and the application entity, in this case, the communication entity serves as an input of the communication process or the communication and application mixture.

Available Option
Available options for the application entity include:
- Application
- What we do
- A short name for application
- Etc.

The Communication & Application Mixture Entity

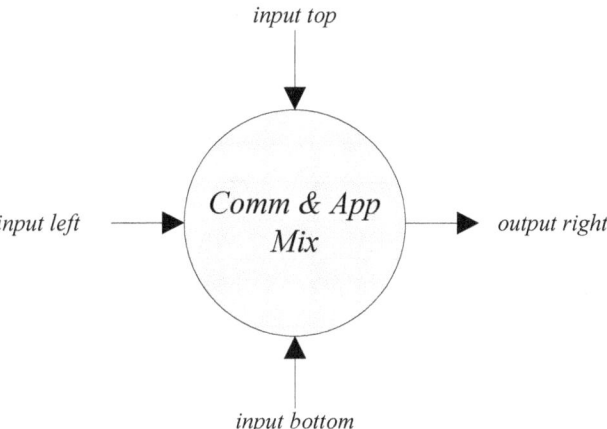

input top

Comm & App
Mix

input left

output right

input bottom

Usage and Description

The communication and the application mixture entity is used to show the mixture of communication and the application. All of the above representations are the same.

The diagram above with the labels is the same as the ones without label. The table below shows more information about the labels; refer to the example section for more information about connecting the communication and application mixture entity.

Input Left	Input Top	Input Bottom	Output Right
Communications	Application	Feedback	Communication and Application

We use the communication and application mixture entity to show the mixture of the communication and our application after being separated. The communication and the application mixture entity takes three inputs; one input is the communication, one input is the application, and the other input which is optional is the feedback. The output of the communication and application mixture entity is connected directly to the communication function entity. The table below shows the output of the communication application mixture entity, based on the input and feedback. Given that our application result depends on communication, in this case we can say the output of this entity is related to the communication input.

Input Left	Input Bottom	Output Right
Green	None	Green
Red	Blue	Green
Red	None	Red

The Error Correction Function Entity

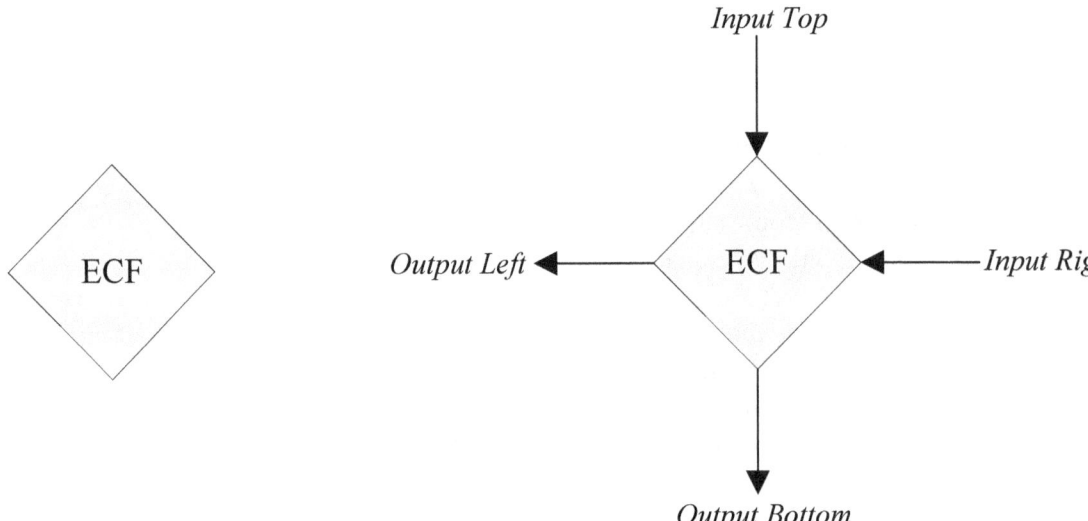

Usage and Description

This is another version of the error correction function entity that takes two inputs and two outputs. The two inputs are the top one and the right one, while the two outputs are the left one and the bottom one. The Error Correction Function (ECF) entity is used to show a correction process. We can use this entity to remove error in our communication process for a top down diagram. The inputs of the ECF related to the outputs can be viewed as follow. The output at the bottom feeds the application, while the one to the left feeds us. The input to the right gets feedback from our parent or the principles, while the one on the top provides the corrected version related to the feedback. The table below shows the inputs outputs result of the ECF.

Input Top	Input Right	Output Left	Output Bottom
Red	Blue	Red	Green

It is always good to look at the ECF entity shows above in a timely manner, since the correction is made at the time the principles are given to us and we apply them. Since the error is occurred at the time we commit it, it makes sense for us to look at the table in a timely manner. With what we have just said, let's look at the table below from the ECF above by taking time into consideration.

Time 1		Time 2	
Input Top	Input Right	Output Left	Output Bottom
Red	Blue	Green	Green

The table below is the same as the one above. It depends on how we look at it.

Time 1		Time 2	
Input Top	Input Right	Output Left	Output Bottom
Red	Blue	Blue	Green

Available Option

Available options for the Error Correction Function includes

- ECF
- Error Correction Function
- Error Correction
- Etc.

The Communication Process Entity

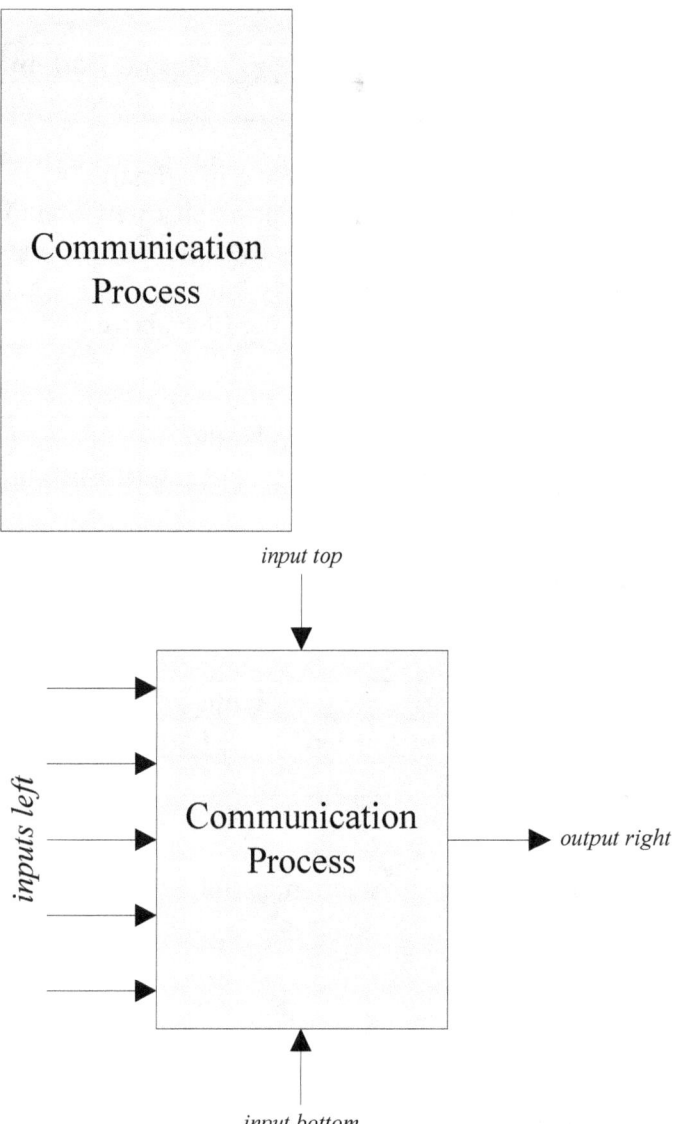

input top

inputs left

Communication
Process

output right

input bottom

Usage and Description

The communication process Entity is the process when we communicate about our application. During the communication process, we communicate about what we are going to do or what we are doing. Since we have a picture of the application in our mind, the communication process is viewed as a mixture of communication and the actual application. We can also say it is a mixture of the overall communication with the application.

The diagram above to the right is the same as the one to the left. In the one to the right, we show the input and the output connections of the communication process. The number of inputs to the left related to the number of people in the communication; see the entity usage section for more information about using the communication process entity. The table below provides more information about the inputs.

Inputs Left	Input Top	Input Bottom	Output Right
Communication	Application	Feedback	Communication and Application

The communication process entity connects the communication and the application. The communication process entity is used when we segment our application to show the actual application from our communication. The communication process connects the application and the parties involve in the communication. The output of the communication process connects to the input of the communication function. The communication process entity is similar to the communication application mixture entity. When using the communication process entity, all the parties that involve in the communication can be considered as inputs. They can be connected directly, however it is always better to provide two inputs to that entity, the communication input and the application input; see the example section for more information about using this entity. The table below shows the output of the communication process entity, related to the communication input and feedback.

Input	Feedback	Output
Green	None	Green
Red	None	Red
Red	Blue	Green

Available Option
Available options for the communication process entity include
- Communication process

- Communication application mixture
- Etc.

The Analysis Window Entity

Analysis Window

Usage and Description
The analysis window entity can be viewed as two entities connected together. It can be viewed as a communication entity with feedback. The way to look at it, the feedback does not show, however it is already included. For example, we can say it is a communication entity, with the principles entity as feedback. The analysis window entity takes communication as input. The output can be connected directly to the application entity to provide and error free application. The table below shows the output of the analysis window entity related to the input.

Input	Output
Green	Green
Red	Green

Available Option
Available options for the analysis window entity include
- Error Correction Function
- ECF
- Error Correction
- Analysis Window
- Error Removal
- Etc.

The Sentence Analysis Entity

Sentence Analysis	Analysis

Usage and Description

The sentence analysis entity is the same as the principles entity. The sentence analysis entity is a feedback entity, it provides error correction mechanism when input to another entity. For example, the sentence analysis entity can be connected to the communication entity, the word entity, etc. to provide feedback or error correction mechanisms. When connected to other entity, the sentence analysis entity provides error correction mechanism to enable them to provide an output without error. For example, if the entity is connected to the communication entity, it allows the output of that entity to be error free. The table bellow shows input output relationship for the entity connected to the sentence analysis entity.

Input	Feedback	Output
Green	None	Green
Red	Blue	Green

Available Option

Available options for the sentence analysis entity include the following

- Sentence Analysis
- Error Analysis
- Analysis
- Communication analysis
- Error Correction Function
- ECF
- Principle
- Etc.

The Communication Result Entity

```
┌─────────────────────┐
│   Communication     │
│      Result         │
└─────────────────────┘
```

Usage and Description

The communication result entity is the result of our application. We can call it communication result we can also call it application result. If we segment our application into several steps to analyze its flow, the communication result is actually the result of the application. The communication result entity always follows the communication function entity. The communication result entity is the output of the communication function entity. We can call it the result of the application or the result of the application execution function. Given that our application result depends on communication, the communication result entity also depends on communication. With that, the communication result entity is related to the communication input as provided by the table below. The output of the column of the table is viewed as the communication result, where the input is communication.

Input	Output
Green	Green
Red	Red

Available Option

Available options for the communication result entity include
- Communication result
- Application result
- Result of what we do
- Result of our communication
- Result of our application
- Project result
- Etc.

The Communication Mixture Entity

 X

Usage and Description
The communication mixture entity is used to group people who involve in the communication. Since the application involves communication, we can also say the communication mixture entity is used to group people who involve in the application. The person entity can be connected directly to the communication mixture entity, and then the communication mixture entity can be connected directly to the communication process entity. Depend of the application; the communication mixture entity can also be used to feed other communication mixture entity; see the entity usage section for more information about using the communication mixture entity. The table below shows the input output relationship of the communication mixture entity. The table below did not take feedback into consideration; however with feedback, the result will be equivalent to the application process entity.

Input	Output
Green	Green
Red	Red

Available Option
Available options for the communication mixture entity include
- Communication Mixture
- Communication process—to some extent
- Comm Mix—shot name
- Etc.

What We Do Entity

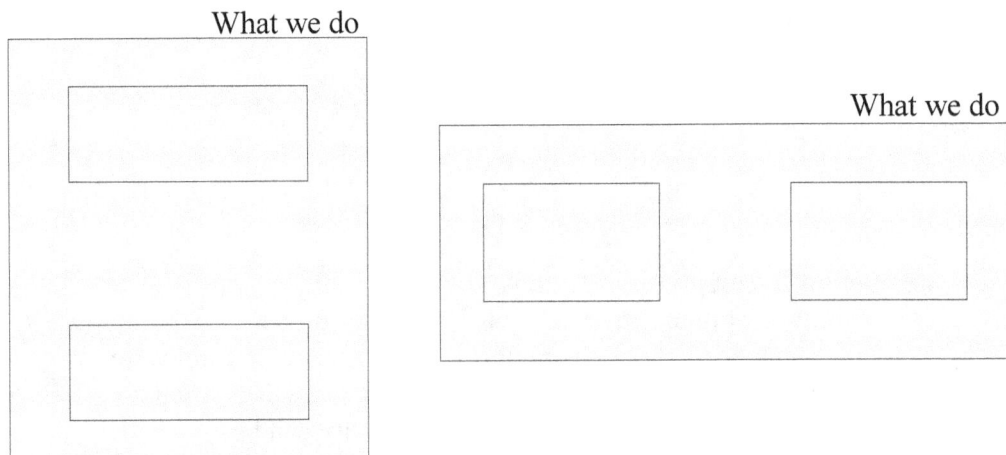

Usage and Description

The what we do entity is simply another way to look at the application entity. The way to look at it, this entity is made of the communication entity and the application entity. It provides an effective way for us to separate our application from communication. This entity provides us the ability to separate what we do from communication. We can either use the top down version or the left to right version. In the top down version, the top entity is considered to be our communication, and the bottom one is our application, which is what we do. In the left to right version, the left entity is considered to be our communication, while the right box is our actual application or simply what we do. The table below shows the result of what we do related to communication.

Communication	What we do
Green	Green
Red	Red

Available Option

Available options for this entity include

- Application
- Our application
- What we do
- What I do
- What you do
- Etc.

The Grouping Entity

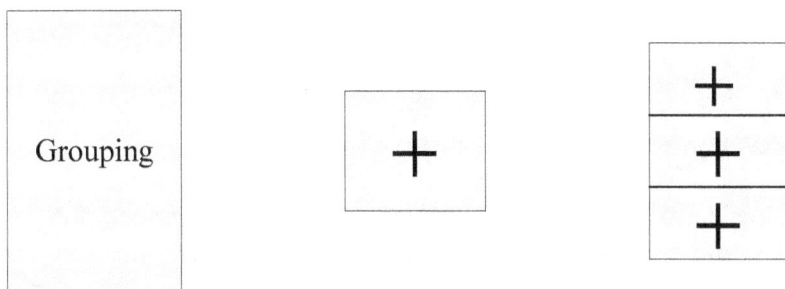

Usage and Description

The grouping entity above is use to group entities like. For example, we can use the grouping entity to group people involves in the application. If our application is made of several parts, we can also use it to group parts of the application. We can use the plus sign or the one with the grouping word, it does not matter. The plus sign with multiple plus can also be used to denote quantity involves in the grouping. Entities like or types can be attached to the grouping entity. Several parts that make up the application can be attached to the grouping entity. Also, mixture of communication can be attached to the grouping entity; see the example section for more information. When communication or communication mixture are attached to the grouping entity, the output of the grouping entity depends on that communication; see the table below for more information.

Input	Output
Green	Green
Red	Red

Available Option

Available options for the grouping entity include
- Grouping
- Addition
- Group
- Plus
- Etc.

The Error Entity

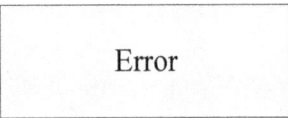

Usage and Description
The error entity can be used to separate error in our communication. In other words, this entity represents the error part of our communication. To show the separation of error in our communication, the error entity can be used to identify that error. For example, if we identify a bad word in our communication, the error entity can be used to identify that word. When the error entity is identified in the communication, the result of the communication which is the application result is related by the table below. In this case, error is identified as red.

The error entity can be used to show error in a typical communication. For instance, in a sentence if a word is flagged as error, the error entity can be used to identify that word. In a sentence that contains error, the error entity can be used to show the error. Given that the analysis process of a sentence involves both the contain of the sentence and the purpose of that sentence, the error entity can be used to show both of them when there is error.

Error	Result
Red	Red

Available Option

Available options for the error entity can also be anything that includes in the communication that causes the error. We mean the identity of anything in the communication that causes the error.

The Compensator Entity

Compensator

Usage and Description

The compensator entity is considered to be extra added to a communication in order to make the communication portable. For instance in a non portable sentence, if one word is flagged as error, if we remove that word and replaced by another word in order to make that sentence portable, the replaced word is viewed as a compensator. Since the analysis of that sentence involves both the function of that sentence and the contain of that sentence, if we add extra to that sentence to adjust the function of that sentence, that extra we add is considered to be a compensator as well.

Available Option

Available options for the compensator entity include anything added to a communication in order to make that communication portable. We mean the identity or the extra that we add to the communication to make it portable.

The Problem Entity

Problem

Usage and Description

While we use a circle with the give rise arrow to show a problem development, as an entity itself, we can use the entity above to show a problem. In this case a problem is an entity like an error is also an entity.

Available Option
Available options for the problem entity include the name of the problem, the name problem, or whatever other name we wan to call it.

The Information Entity

```
Information
```

Usage and Description
The information entity can be used to show the contain of the communication. This entity can be connected to other entities. Error analysis can also be performed on the information entity to determine the correctness of the information. In that chase, the information entity can be connected to other entities. For example, the error analysis entity can be connected to the information entity, to determine the correctness of the information. In this case, the result of the information is related to that table.

Feedback	Information
Blue	Green
None	Red

Available Option
Available options for the information entity include
- Information
- History
- Story
- Novel
- Article
- News
- Etc.

The Feedback Entity

```
┌─────────────────────────────────┐
│                                 │
│          Feedback               │
│                                 │
└─────────────────────────────────┘
```

Usage and Description
While the feedback entity may not be needed, however it can be used if necessary to show a given or specific feedback. The feedback entity is simply principle given that can be applied to correct specific error. The feedback entity is the same as analysis, principles, and ECF.

The Action Entity

```
┌─────────────────────────────────┐
│                                 │
│            Action               │
│                                 │
└─────────────────────────────────┘
```

Usage and Description
The action entity can be used for problem statement. For instance, before we start our application or project, we can use the action entity flow connection to show our problem statement. The action entity can be used to show our problem statement. For example, to use the action entity, we can attach a person entity to its input, and the output can be attached to the reason entity. The action entity can also take analysis as feedback to determine the result of the action. We can feedback the action entity with the error analysis entity to make sure the action result is error free. The table below shows the output of the action entity, related to the input and feedback.

Input	Feedback	Output
Green	None	Green
Red	Blue	Green
Red	None	Red

Available Option
Available options for the action entity include the following
- Action
- Function
- This, That
- Etc.

The Reason Entity

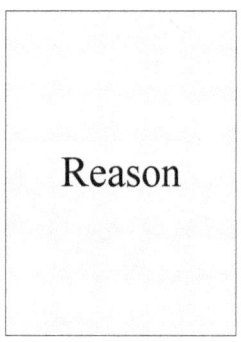

Usage and Description
The reason entity is to be used with the action entity for problem statement. For instance, the reason entity can be used with the action entity to determine the result of the action.

The reason entity is considered to the output of the action entity. We can also say that the reason entity is the result of the action entity. The reason entity answers the following question; why are we taking this action? Why are we performing this action? What problem do we solve by performing this action? The reason entity which is the output of the action entity is the result of the communication and the feedback in the action entity; the table below shows the result. Rather than using communication to show the result, in this case we use action and result; where the action determines the reason.

Action	Reason
Green	Green
Red	Red

Available Option

Available options for the reason entity include

- Reason
- Solve Problems
- Result
- Provide Solutions
- Etc.

The Entity Element

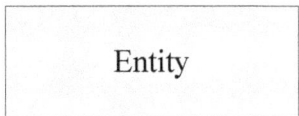

Entity

Usage and Description

The entity element can be used to represent an entity. It can also be used to represent elements. Another way to look at it, we can use the entity element to represent a physical entity. The entity element can be used to represent any actual entity. As we have just said, the entity element can be used to represent entities or elements. For instance we can use the element to represent a physical entity. We can also use it to represent a non physical entity. By representing an entity, we can simply put the name of that entity in the element.

Since the function of an entity is also an entity, it is possible to use the entity element to show an *entity as a function*. For instance, if we identify a function, then we can use the entity element to show that actual function. In this case, we can have something like this. Assume that we identify *Function 1*, and then *Function 1* is viewed as a function of an entity. In this case, we can show it like the diagram below, where *entity 1* is viewed as the actual entity and *function 1* is viewed as the actual function.

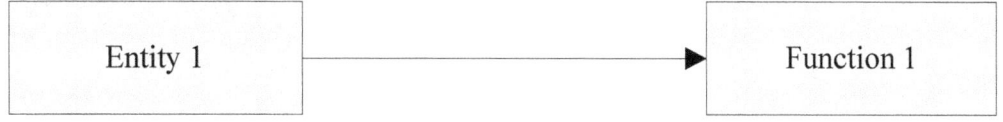

Since the aspect of an entity is also an entity, the entity element can also be used to show the aspect of an entity. In this case, it is being used to show an *entity as aspect*. Assume that we identify an entity, since the aspect of that entity is also an entity, then we can use the entity element to show that aspect as follow. Let's say we identify *Entity 1*, where *Entity 1* has *Aspect 1*, and then we can use the entity element to show that in the form below. In this case, *Entity 1* is the actual entity, where *Aspect 1* is the actual aspect of that entity and it is also an entity.

Available Option
Available options for the entity element include
- Entity
- Element
- Physical entity
- Non physical entity
- Name of the entity
- Item
- Thing
- Any thing
- Function
- Function of entity
- Aspect
- Aspect of entity
- Etc.

The Communication Element Entity

Communication Element

Usage and Description

The communication element entity represents a communication entity. We can say that the communication element represents communication entities that are not word, sentence, and paragraph. While we use the term communication element, we can also use the term communication entity as well. The communication element entity can be used to represent communication entity. For instance, we can use the communication entity element to represent pictures, images, videos, drawings, diagrams etc.

While we say that the communication element entity is used to represent communication elements that are not words, sentences, and paragraphs, however since words, sentences and paragraphs are considered to be communication elements, the communication element entity can be used to represent them as well.

Available Option

Available options for the communication element include

- Picture, photo
- Image
- Video
- Drawing, diagram
- Chart, flow chart
- Graph, table
- Audio
- Voice
- Word, sentence, paragraph
- Book, journal, news paper, magazine, video, video,
- Etc.

The ECF Entity

ECF

Usage and Description

This short ECF entity version is considered as an error correction entity. The way to look at it, this entity can be connected to other entities to send a correction signal to that entity to enable an error free output. As we say above, the ECF entity can be connected as feedback to other entities to send signals to them to enable them to correct any error that is presented. For example, this entity can be connected to the communication process entity to enable the output of the communication process entity to be error free. When this entity is connected to an entity, it sends a blue signal to that entity. The table below shows the input output relationship of the connected entity related to the ECF entity. From the table below, in the fourth row, ECF None means no presence of ECF.

Connected Entity	ECF	Output
Green	None	Green
Red	Blue	Green
Red	None	Red

Available Option

Available options for the ECF entity includes

- Error Correction Function
- ECF
- Analysis Logic
- Principles
- Sentence Analysis
- Error Correction
- Parent Principles
- Etc.

The Definition Entity

Definition

Usage and Description

By understanding the entity element, the word entity, and the information entity; the definition entity may not be needed and it is not needed in our model. Since word 1 points to entity 1 and definition 1 points to entity 1, so it is not needed to show the definition entity in a model.

The Separation Line Entity

|

|

|

|

|

|

Usage and Description

We can use the separation line to separate the steps of our application process. We can also use it to show the separation of our application from communication. The way to look at it, from start to finish, we can use this line to show the step we undertake from the starting of our application to the finish of our application. We can use this line to show the separation and provide more information about each step.

We can also use the separation line to show entity separation, for instance words separation in sentences, sentences separation in paragraphs etc. After we have identified some entities within a group, we can use the separation line to separate each entity. After we have identified entities that make up our communication, we can use the separation line to separate the entities or communication elements. Using the separation line is important, since it enables us to concentrate in the area of our interest during the analysis.

The separation line can also be used to show steps in a relationship diagram. For instance, we can use the separation line and the time line to show steps in a relationship diagram related to time. Refer to the example section for more information.

Available Option
Available options for the separation line include
- Separation
- Process separation
- Step separation
- Domain separation
- Communication and application separation
- Entity separation line
- Element separation line
- Item separation line
- Etc.

The Time Line Entity

Usage and Description
Similarly to the separation line, if desired time line can be used to show function execution or specific event related to time. For instance, we can use timeline to show specific communication at a given time; see the example section for more information. Above, the diagram to the left

shows the first timeline, while the one to the right shows subsequent timeline.

Available Option
Available options for the time line include
- Time line name
- Date
- Time
- Subsequent timeline or subsequent line
- Date line
- Etc.

The Progress Entity

Usage and Description
The progress entity or progress line can also be used to show the progress of a function or the progress of our communication in our project. We can use the progress entity to show the progress of our application function execution. We can also use the progress bar to show the progress of the overall project we are working on.

Available Option
Available options for the progress bar include
- % of completed on time
- Progress related to time
- Progress line
- Progress entity
- Etc.

The Error in Communication Gives Rise Entity

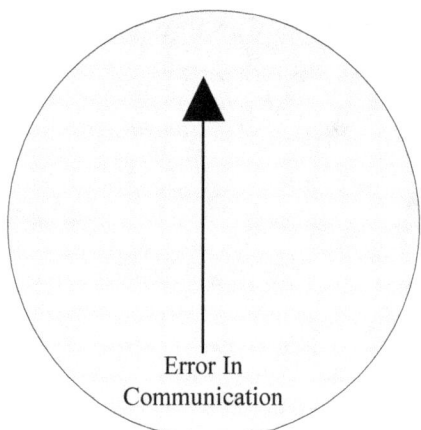

Error In
Communication

Description and Usage

Given that our application is communication driven and when we commit error in communication it affects our application, this entity or diagram can be used to show the result of our application related to error in communication. This diagram can be filled to show the result of the application based on error. By tracking error in our communication, if there is a problem in our application, at the end we can use this entity to show that problem.

The Work Entity

This entity can be used to construct the communication related to work diagram. Since our project is communication driven, we can show how people work together related to communication. In this case, it makes sense for us to show that in a circular form. By using the work entity with the arrows, we can construct a circular diagram to show how we work together from our communication.

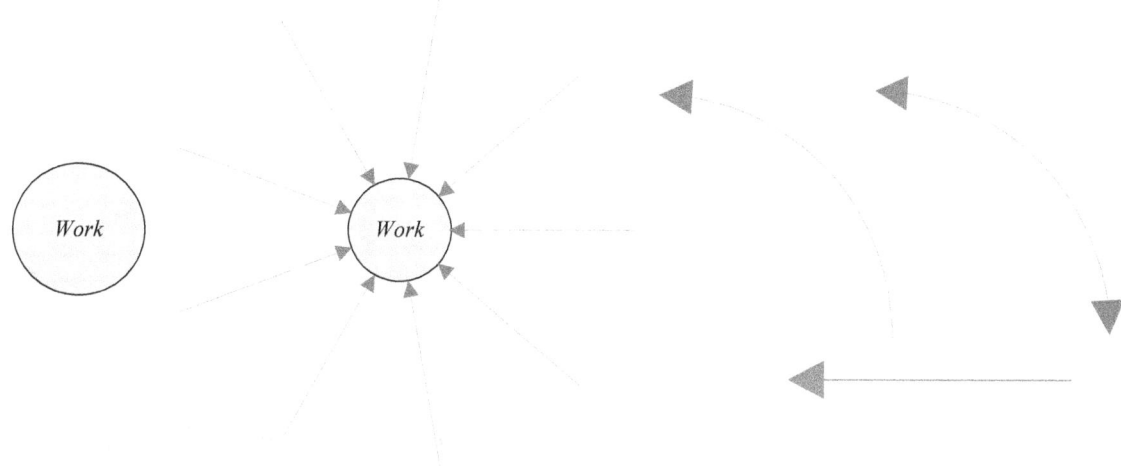

Available Option

Available options for the work entity include

- Work
- What we do
- Etc.

Assume that we have two people working in a project. We know that those two people communicate together to do their works, in this case, we can use the work entity to construct a diagram to show the flow of the communication of those people related to what they do. Using the diagram below, we simply show two people communicate together to do what they do.

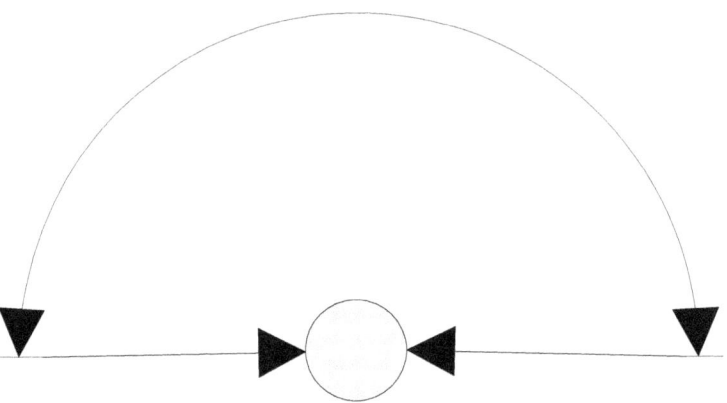

Using the same diagram above, we can add another person to the project. In this case, we have three people working together. The communication of those people is what enables them to work together. In this case, we can simply show that in a circular form as shown below. The diagram below shows communication of three people related to work.

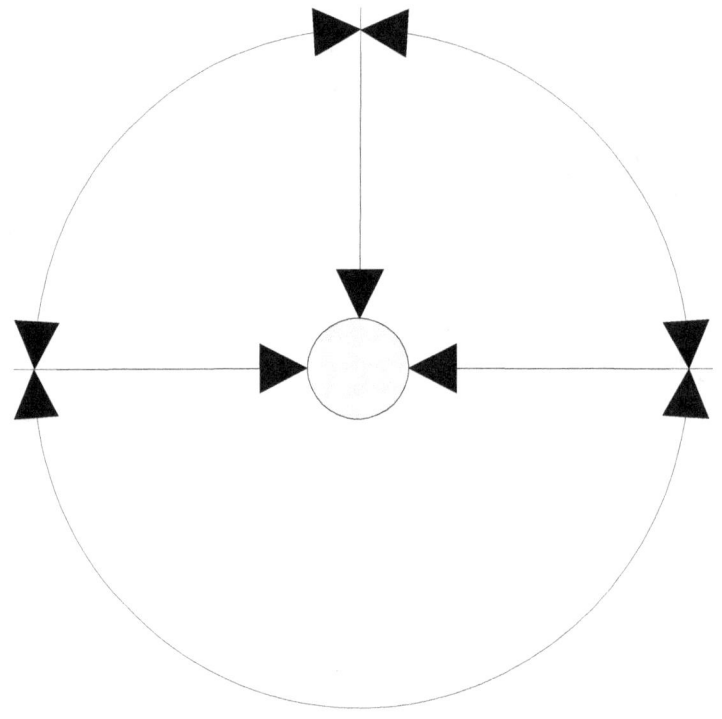

Assume that we have four people communicate together to do their works, we can then extend the work together diagram to show that. In this case, we can show the people communicate together to do their works as shown below.

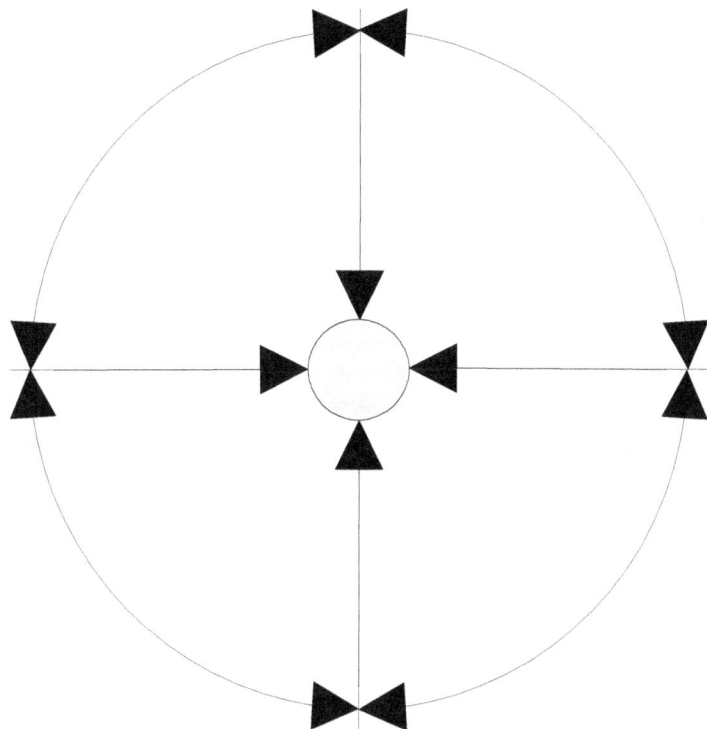

We can simply name the two arrows below communication related to work arrow. We use the arc arrow to show communication from person to person, while we use the straight arrow to show what a person does in relation to communication. The communication related to work arrow can be used to construct the diagram of the communication related to work and to show the flow of the communication in that diagram. As we previously said, the arrow to the left shows the flow of communication from person to person, while the one to the right shows the flow of the communication related to the function or the purpose of the communication. In other words, the one to the right shows the flow of the communication related to what we do.

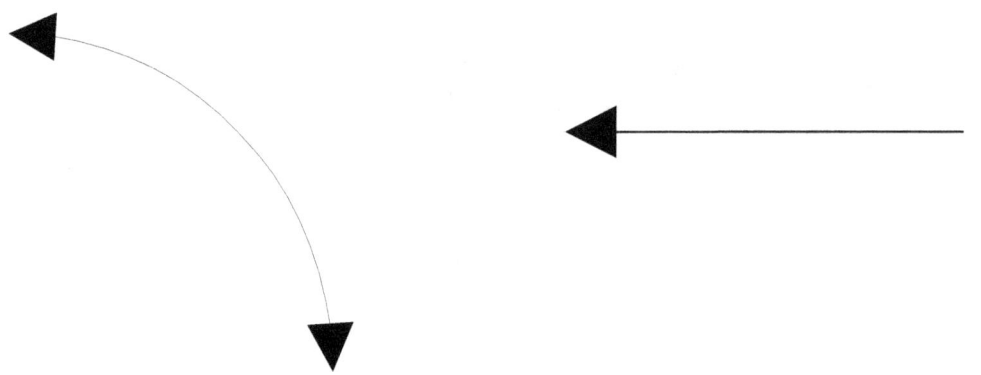

Time Chart and Dateline Entity

Time line can be used in conjunction with dateline to record events, statements, questions etc. Below we show a timeline and a dateline that can be connected together to show record of statement; see the entity usage section for more information.

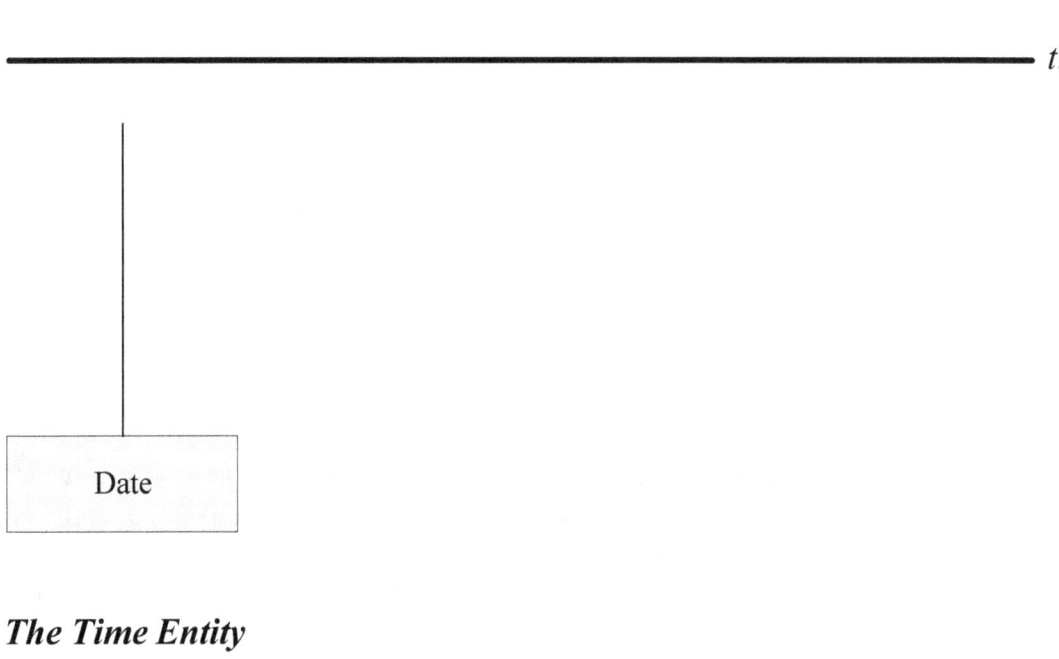

time

Date

The Time Entity

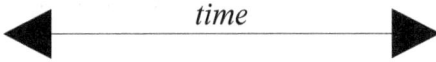

time

Usage and Description

Assume that we are using the time chart with the date line where we want to show the difference between the two dates, we can use the time entity to show that. For instance, if we want to show how long it takes from the first date to the second date, we can use the time entity to show that. We use the time entity to show time or exact time between two dates or times.

The Operating Principle Line Entity

Usage and Description

The operating principle line entity can be used with the principle entity and the person entity to show the principle the people in an application depend on. Refer to the example section for more information about the usage of the operating principle line entity.

The Sub Function Entity

```
┌─────────────────────┐
│                     │
│         Sub         │
│      Function       │
│                     │
├─────────────────────┤
└─────────────────────┘
```

Usage and Description

It is always possible for a project to be divided into different sections, where the main function of the project is made of many other functions. In this case, it is always possible to have sub functions. A sub function can be considered as a function that is a part of the main function. It can also be considered as an external function. Assume that a project is divided into several sections, where each section is managed by a different person; it is possible for each of those sections to be set as a sub function. While smaller groups of people tend to be easier to manage, using sub functions is considered to be a better way of managing a project. The way to look at it, if the communication includes several functions where some of those functions are embedded inside other functions, the sub function entity can be used to show functions that are included inside other functions. Below shows the communication function and it is made of tree functions.

Communication Function

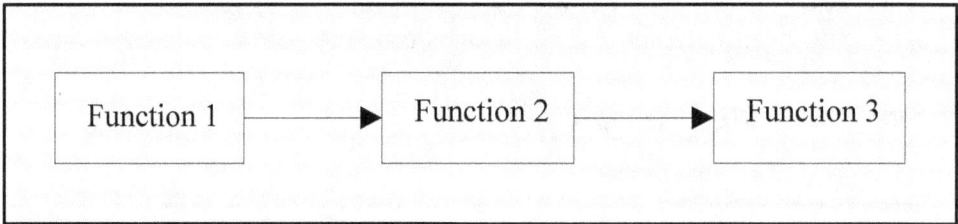

The diagram below shows *function 1* which is a part of the communication function and it contains other functions inside.

Function 1

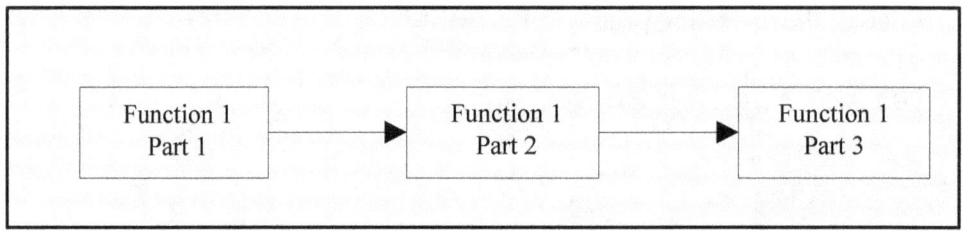

Functions that are considered as sub functions can be identified as the following; in this case, *function 1* contains other functions inside. We use the extra line inside *function 1* near the bottom to indicate that *function 1* is a sub function or *function 1* contains other functions inside.

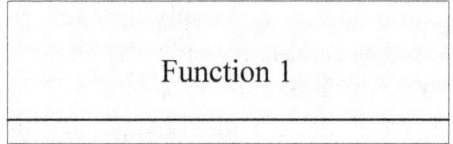

Since the communication function is denoted as $f(x)$, in this case we can use indexing to denote part of the communication when the communication function is divided into several parts. For instance, assume that our communication function is made of 3 parts as shown by the diagram above, then we can represent them in the form of $f_1(x)$, $f_2(x)$, and $f_3(x)$ as shown by the diagram below.

$$f(x)$$

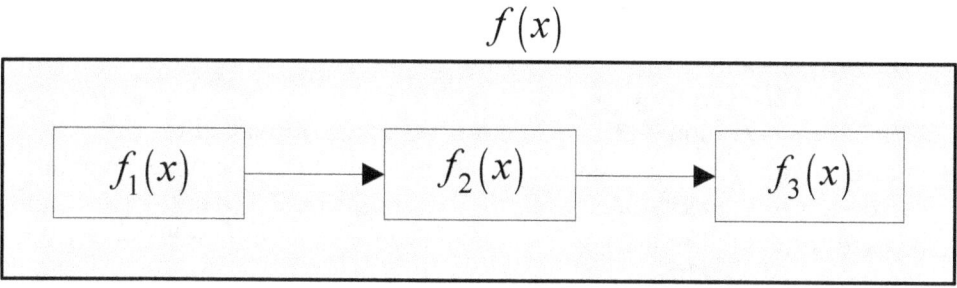

By understanding the explanation and the figure above, we can also use indexing and summation to represent our communication function when our communication function is made of several parts. For instance the communication function from the diagram above can be represented in the form of

$$f(x) = f_1(x) + f_2(x) + f_3(x)$$

In term of indexing and summation; assume that our communication function is made of N parts, and then we have

$$f(x) = \sum_{n=1}^{N} f_n(x)$$

The Notes Entity

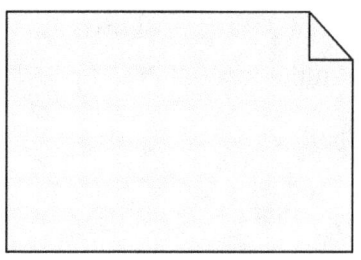 

Usage and Description

When using a computer, sometime it is necessary to take note. For instance, within a project screen on a computer, it may be necessary for a person to use a sticky note as a reminder; in this case, the note entity can be used for that. The note entity can be used on a computer screen to show user's notes. Both of the entities shown above are the same. Users can use them to show or hold their notes. The note entity can also be used on paper or board if desired. For instance, within our project, we can use it as a reminder.

Available Option

Available options for the note entity include
- Note
- Note entity
- Note holder
- Sticky note
- Etc.

The Node Entity

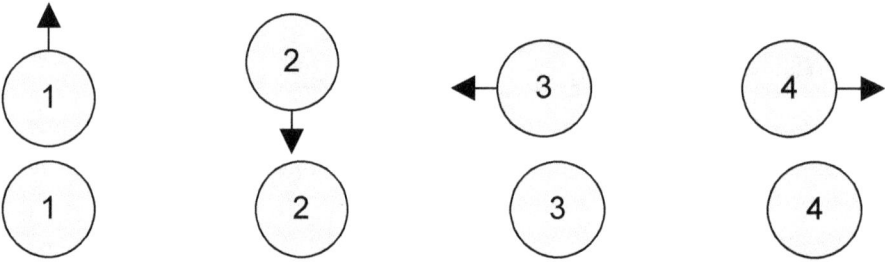

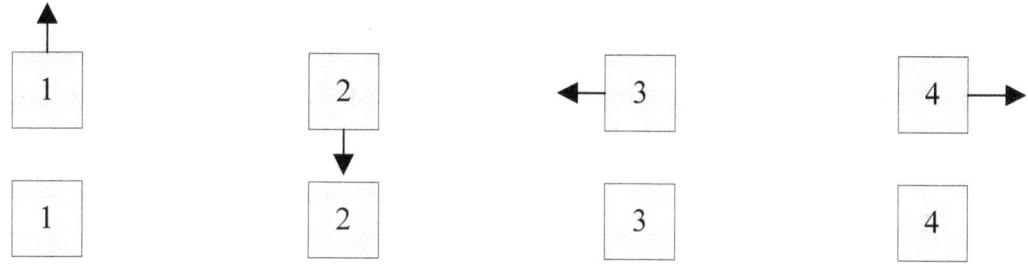

Usage and Description

Within a communication or conversation, a node is considered to be an important point of that communication or that conversation. We can also say that a node is a point of interest of a communication. We can flag specific point in a communication and assign a node to it. From the diagram above, we show the nodes both in square form and circle form. As shown above, nodes can also be shown with or without arrow as longer they are placed properly. Refer to the entity usage section for more information about using the node entity.

Available Option

Available options for the node entity include
- Node
- Node number
- Point
- Point number
- Location
- Location number
- Communication Node
- Information Node
- Specific location
- Etc.

Nodes can also be used to show continuity from one point to another point. In other words, we can use the node entity to show continuity from one location to another location. For instance, we can use node number to show the continuity of a relationship or specific entity at specific point. Let's assume that we have *Entity 1* is related to *Entity 2*, and that relationship is related to the relationship of *Entity 3* and *Entity 4*. Now, if in a piece of paper or drawing board we cannot fit all of it, then we can place a node number in that part, then continue by putting another node number to another piece of paper or in another part of the same sheet or in another part of a drawing board or another drawing board to show the continuity of that relationship as shown by this diagram.

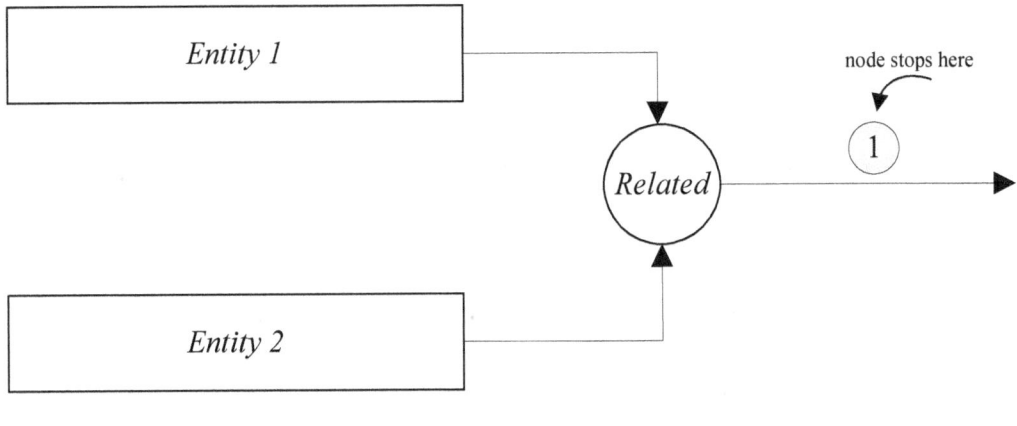

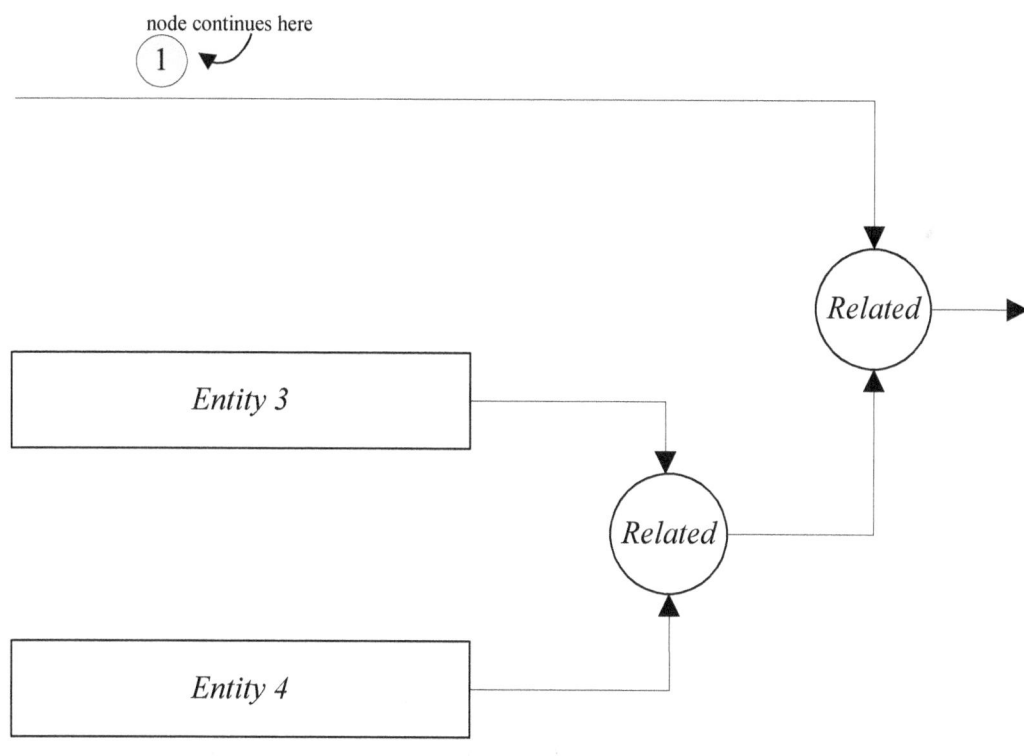

sheet 2 or part 2 of sheet 1

The node entity can also be used in a relationship to identify an entity at specific node, where that entity can be defined and identified by that node. Refer to the example section for more information about defining and identify an entity at a node in a given relationship.

The Callout Entity

Usage Description

Callout can be used to show information at specific point. Instead of using the node entity to show node number then give information of that node, the callout entity can be used instead to show specific information at that point. Overall we use the callout entity to record section of interest in our communication or conversation. Refer to the example section for more information about using the callout entity.

Available Option

Available options for the callout entity include

- Callout
- Callout entity
- Information point
- Node information
- Etc.

The Node Information Table Entity

Node Number	1	2	3
Node Information			

Usage and Description

When using the node entity, it is possible for us to provide information about the nodes we identify. By using the node table, we can provide information about the nodes. The node table information is made of node number and node information. For instance if within our project diagram we record node number 1 in our communication, it makes sense to provide more information about node number 1 or the communication at that point. By using the node table information, we can provide more information for that node. Refer to the example section to learn more about using the node information table.

Available Option

Available options for the node information table include
- Node information table
- Table
- Information table
- Information table at specific locations
- Etc.

The Communication Holder Entity

Communication Holder

Usage and Description

As we have learned previously, our project can be divided into different sections, where each section is managed by a different person. When that happens, it may be possible for an employee in a project to work in two sections. For instance in a project, *function 1* is considered to be the main function for *employee 1* and that employee is managed by *manger 1*. Within that same project, *manager 2* is managed *function 2* and need some help from *employee 1*. Now, *employee 1* is working in both *function 1* and *function 2*, but managed by both *manger 1* and *manger 2*. We assume that *function 2* is a sub function within the project. When viewing on the screen or paper, it is not practical to show double representation of *employee 1*. In this case, if the sub function is open within the main function, then *employee 1* is replaced by his/her respective communication holder in *function 2*. It is very important to understand the communication holder entity and look at it in a practical approach. In life a person cannot be duplicated. It is not possible to see double representation of a person. For this reason, the communication holder is important, since it allows one person to work on multiple sections of a project, but can never be seen or viewed as duplicate. Refer to the example section to learn more about using the communication holder entity.

Available Options
Available options for the communication holder entity include the following
- Communication Holder
- Information Holder
- Conversation Holder
- Etc.

The External Communication Holder Entity

> External
> Communication Holder

Usage and Description
Since the result of our project is a function of communication, it is very important for us not tot take communication for granted. While working in a project, it may be possible for us to use communication or information

from people that are not physically in that project. By using the external communication holder, we make it possible to use communication from people that are not physically in our project. This is the way to look at it, assume that we are working in a project where we need information to accomplish what we are doing. The information we need can be from a person that is not in the project, a magazine article, newsletter, etc. By using the external communication holder, we can include those entities in the project, but externally. In other words, we use those communications in the project, but they are not from people who are physically in the project. In this case, we simply represent them as external communication holders. Refer to the example section to learn more about using the external communication holder entity.

Available Options
Available options for the external communication holder include the following
- Person name, people
- Article, magazine article, radio program, TV program, Journal etc.
- Book, magazine, program, newspaper, newsletter
- Website, web page
- Email, mail
- Etc.

The Empty Container Entity

Usage and Description
The empty container entity can be used to group parts of application, parts of communication function, and parts of application result. The first diagram below shows the usage of the empty container entity to group some parts of the communication functions. The second diagram shows the usage of the empty container to group some parts of the application,

while the third diagram shows the usage the empty container to group some parts of the application result. In this case we assume the overall application result is made of different parts. Depends where we place the empty container, we can give it the following names: part of application container, part of communication function container, and part of application result container. Refer to the entity usage section form more information and example about using the empty container entity.

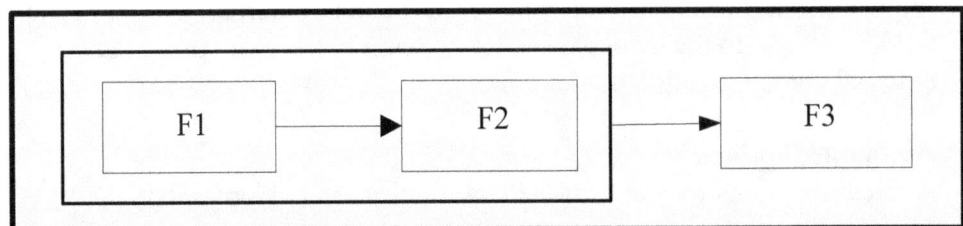

Communication Function

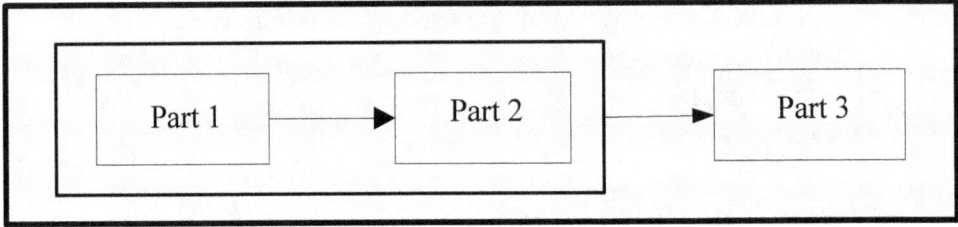

Application

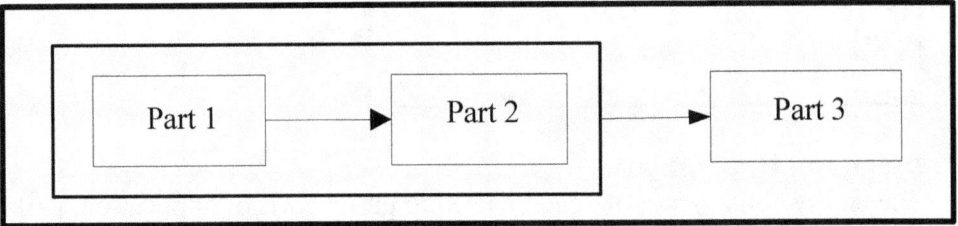

Application Result

Available Option
Available options for the empty container entity include

- Empty Container

- Part container
- Function container
- Result Container
- Application container
- Empty container
- Etc.

The Reference Entity

Reference

Usage and Description
Within our project diagram, if it is needed, the reference entity can be used to show references. For instance in our project diagram, it might be possible for us to link to another page, in this case we can use the reference entity for that. The reference entity can also be used to provide reference information. Since not all entities are considered to be references, it maybe possible for a reference to undergo the same analysis as a regular entity. Although references are principles themselves; but in order for that to happen, the principles must be understood. In the events that the principles are not understood, it is possible for an indicated entity that claims to be a reference, but not identified as a reference at all. To determine that, analysis can be used to analyze an entity to determine if it is a reference or not; as shown by the table below; refer to the example section for more information about using the reference entity.

Input	Feedback	Output
Green	None	Green
Red	None	Red
Red	Blue	Green

Available Option
Available options for the reference entity include
- Reference

- Reference entity
- Reference information
- Reference information
- Link information
- Etc.

The Question Entity

Question

Usage and Description

The question entity is used to show a question. Since questions are parts of communication, during our communication it is possible for us to ask questions to each other. The question entity is used during a communication to indicate a question. Since questions are parts of communication and they undergo the same analysis as communication, feedbacks can be given for an asked question. The following table shows the result of a question with and without feedback.

Input	Feedback	Output
Green	None	Green
Red	None	Red
Red	Blue	Green

Available Option

Available options for the question entity include
- Question
- Inquire
- Query
- Part of communication
- Communication element
- Communication entity
- Etc.

The Answer Entity

Answer

Usage and Description

The answer entity is used to show the answer of a question. Since answers of questions are part of communication, during our communication it is possible for us to ask questions and answer questions to each other. The answer entity can be used during our communication to indicate the answer of a question. Since answers are parts of communication, they undergo the same analysis as regular communication. During the answer of a question, feedbacks can be given to determine the correctness of that answer. In this case, the feedbacks enable us to determine if the underlined entity is an answer or not. The following table show the result of an answer related to feedback.

Input	Feedback	Output
Green	None	Green
Red	None	Red
Red	Blue	Green

Available Option

Available option for the answer entity include

- Answer
- Response
- Reply
- Part of communication
- Communication clcmcnt
- Communication entity
- Etc.

Unknown Entity

Usage and Description

Since we communicate relatively with entities that we identify, during our communications, it may not be possible for us to identify unknown entities. Since not all of us understand the principles of communication during our communications, it may be possible for some of us to talk or communicate about entities that we don't know—do not identify—or do not exist. When that happens, it makes sense for us to analyze that communication to ask questions about those entities or whether they point to actual entities. In this case, it is possible for us to request information on whether words that refer to those entities point to actual entities. In this case, we can have something like this.

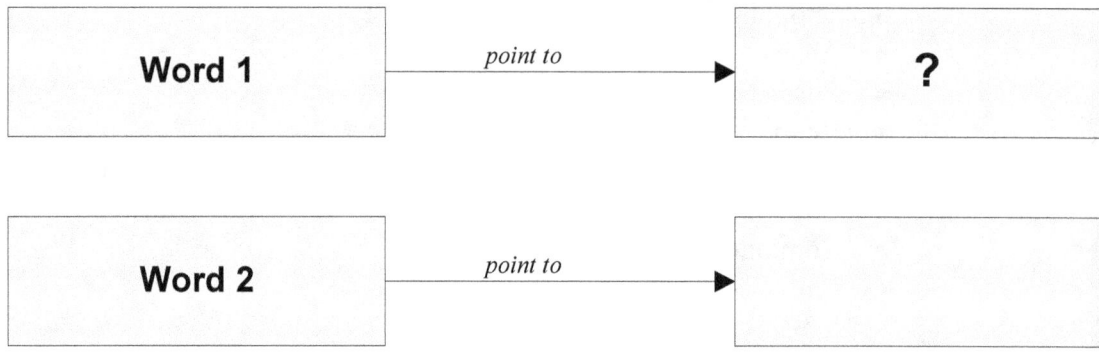

As shown above, the first diagram means what entity *Word 1* points to, while the second diagram means *Word 2* points to a blank entity. Since the there is no such as blank entity, in this case the blank entity refers to an entity that does not exist in the communication.

In addition to the way we have it above, it is possible for us to use cross an entity to show an entity that does not exist. By doing so, we can have the form below

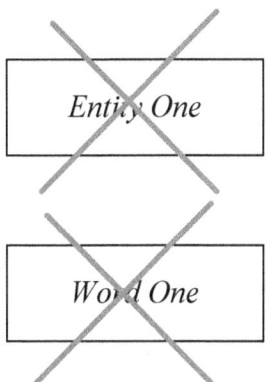

Number Identification

#1   #2   #3

#etc.

Usage and Description

During communication, it is possible for us to separate or identify an entity and refer to it by a number. In order to do that, we can use the # identification with any number to label an entity or refer to it.

The Information Label

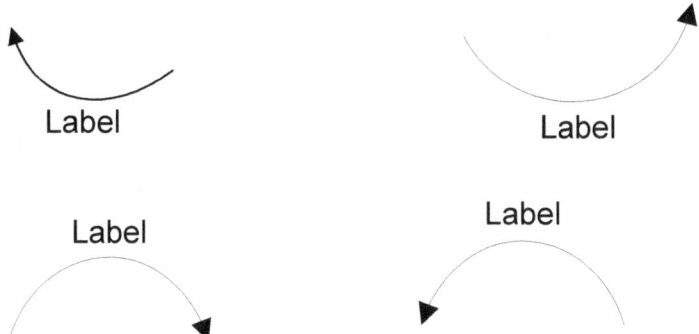

Label   Label

Label   Label

Usage and Description

The information label can be used to show more information about entities. The following labels can be used to show more information about entities identification. We can use them to add more information on entities or simply to identify more information of entities. The labels can be positioned to locations of our interest. For instance, they can be flipped and rotated to reflect a desired position.

The Point to Label

Usage and Description

Since when we see or repeat a word we think about what that word represents, the point to label enables us to identify an entity that is represented by a word. For instance, we use the point to label to show a word that is represented by an entity or physical entity. We can also use the point to label to show a communication entity that points to an actual entity. Refer to the example section for more information about using the point to label.

Available Option
Available options for the point to label include:
- Point to
- Define
- Define from
- Define by
- Map to
- Mean
- Identify
- Identify by
- Point to arrow
- Word point to entity label
- Word point to entity information
- Word to entity information label
- Point to entity
- Point to actual entity
- Show
- Etc.

The Give Rise Label

Usage and Description
The give rise label can be used to show an entity that gives rise to another entity. For instance, we have used the give rise arrow to show how a

problem developed from error in communication. In this case, we use it to show a problem development process where a problem is derived from a communication error.

Available Option
Available options for the give rise arrow include:
- Give rise
- Derive from
- Develop from
- Derive by
- Give rise entity
- Become
- Cause
- Come form
- Turn to
- Etc.

The Relationship Label
We can use the relationship label to show an entity that is related to another entity. We can rotate the label to change its position accordingly. We can also change the text to reflect to what we are doing.

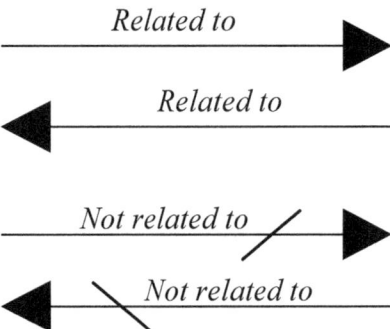

Available Option
Available options for the relationship label include:
- Relate
- Link

- Connect
- Part of
- Has
- Contain
- Etc.

The By Label

We know that the relationship between two entities is also an entity; we can use the by label to identify that entity. In other words, we use the by label to identify the relationship between two entities. Let's say it again; the purpose of this label is to identify entities that serve as relationships between other entities. For instance if entity 1 is related to entity 2 and we identify the relationship entity as entity 3, we can use the by label to identify that entity. In this case, we can simply put it in a form like entity 1 *related to* entity 2 *by* entity 3. The label can be rotated and flipped accordingly. The text can also be changed accordingly as well.

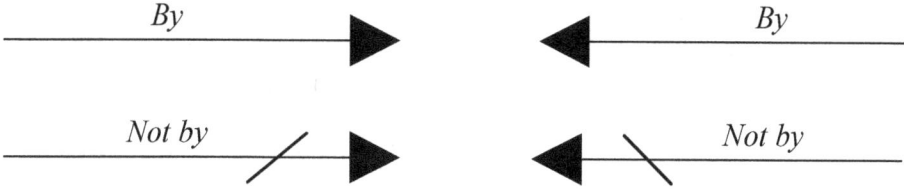

Available Option

Available options for the by label include:

- By
- By this
- By that
- Connected by to some extent
- Linked by to some extent
- Etc.

The Dependency Label

The dependency label is used to show an entity that depends on another entity. Since a given entity can depend to another entity, it is possible for us to use the dependency entity to show that. For instance, if *entity one* depends on *entity two*, then we can use the dependency label to show that *entity one* depends on *entity two*.

Available Option
Available option for the dependency label include
- Depend
- Related
- Dependency entity
- Etc.

The Agreement Label
The agreement label is used to show an entity that agrees with another entity. Since we communicate relatively about entities that we identify and the communications about those entities depend on them rather than us personally, it is possible for us to show the agreement of an entity with another entity during our communication. We can use the agreement label to show that. For instance, if a communication agrees with an entity, then the agreement label can be used to show that. If the answer of a question agrees with specific information, then the agreement label can be used to show that.

Available Options
Available option for the agreement label include

- Agree
- Match
- Related
- Etc.

The Match Label

The match label can be used to show an entity that matches with another entity. Since communication about specific information must match that information, during our communication about specific information, it is possible for us to use the match label to show that our communication matches the actual information.

Available Option

Available options for the match label include

- Match
- Related
- Agree
- Point to
- Go with
- Map
- Etc.

The Inclusion Label

The inclusion label can be used to show an entity that includes in another entity. Since an entity can be made of several entities, then it is possible for us to use the inclusion label to show that. Since the function of an entity is also an entity, the inclusion label can also be used to show a function that includes other functions. For instance, if *Entity One* includes *Entity Two*, then the inclusion label can be used to show *Entity One* contains *Entity Two*.

has ➤   does not have ⫽ ➤

Available Option

Available options for the inclusion label include

- Has/have
- Includes/include
- Contains/contain
- Inclusion entity
- Part of
- Exist with
- Given with or is given with
- Is a part of
- Contain
- Etc.

The Attach Label

The attach label or the attach entity can be used to show an entity that is attached to another entity. For instance, if an entity connects to another entity, then the attach label can be used to show that. We can position the attach label to our desired orientation.

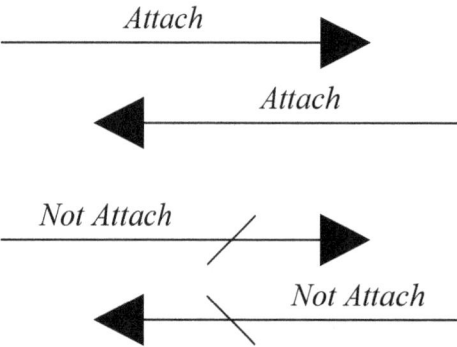

Available Option

Available options for the attach label include

- Attach

- Connect
- Match entity
- Etc.

The Interaction Label

The interaction label can be used to show the interaction of an entity. For instance, we can use the interaction label to show the interaction of a person with an entity. Since information about an entity points to that entity, the interaction of an entity points to that entity as well. In this case, the interaction label can be used in conjunction with another entity to show the interaction of an entity with another entity.

Available Option

Available options for the interaction label include
- Interaction
- Interaction entity
- Interact
- Use
- Etc.

Some Communication Related to Work Labels

The following labels can be use to construct the communication related to work diagram. We can annotate the labels with words that we like. For instance, the *communication to* can be replaced by *talk to*, *speak to* etc.

The Use Label

The use label is used to show an entity that uses another entity; for instance if *Entity One* uses *Entity Two*, then we can use the use label to show that. In this case, while *Entity One* uses *Entity Two*, however *Entity One* is not always a part of *Entity Two*.

Communication Signals Direction

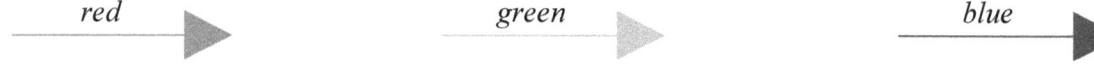

The communication signals direction arrows can be used to show the signal flow of our communication. For instance, the red arrow can be used to show the flow of a negative communication, the green a can be used to show the flow of a positive communication, while the blue arrow can be used to show the flow a communication that is considered as feedback.

Curl Braces

If necessary or needed, it may be possible for us to use curl braces for annotation in our diagrams. The curl braces below can be used to provide more information with an entity.

The Relationship Entity

While it may not be necessary, since the relationship between two entities is also an entity, the relationship entity below can be used to show that. The relationship entity is given in this form.

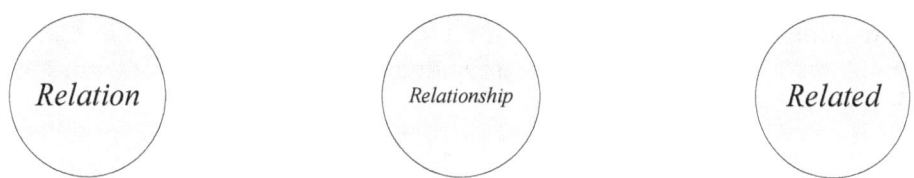

Usage Information

Assume that entity 1 is related to entity 2 by entity 3, since the relationship of two entities is also entity, the relationship entity can be used in the form below to show that. We can say that entity 3 is the result of the relationship of entity 1 and entity 2.

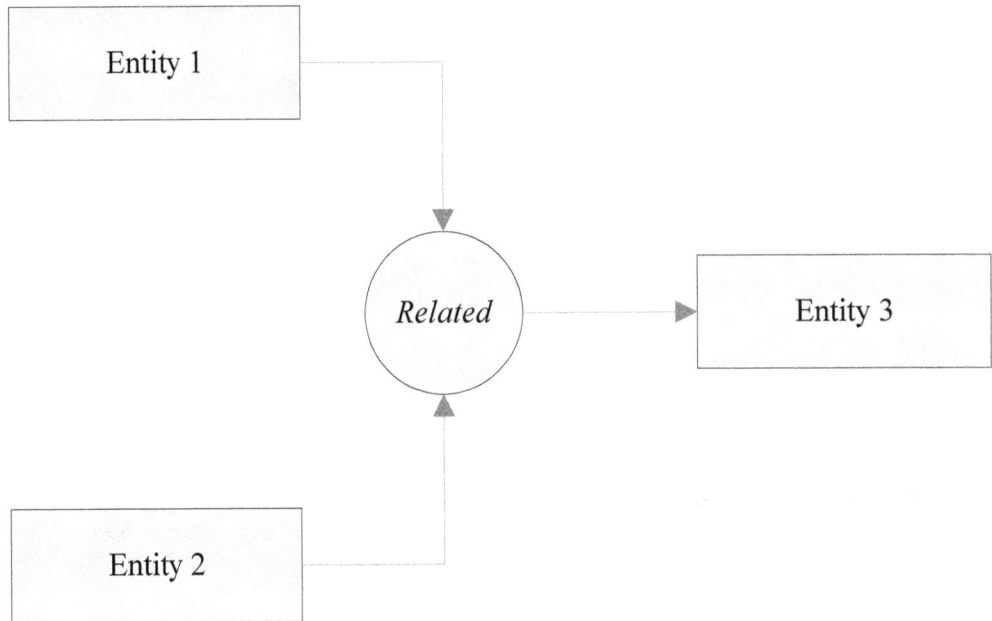

The relationship entity can also be used for multiple relationships in the form below. Assume that there is a relationship with entity 3 and entity 4, in this case we have

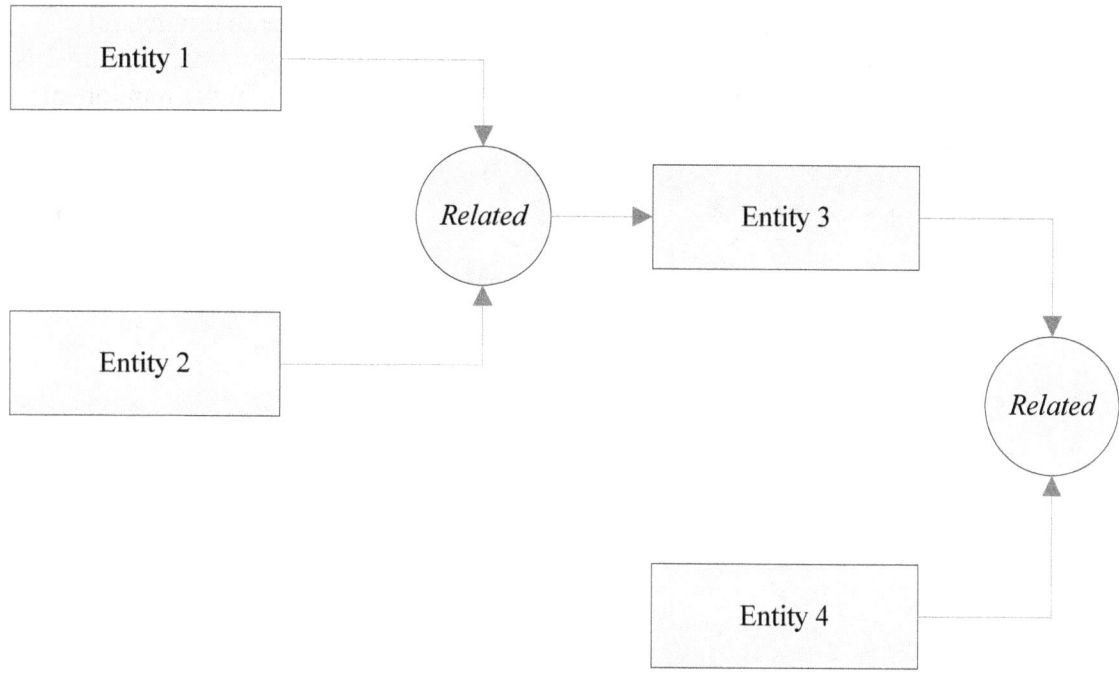

Now since the relationship between entity 3 and entity 4 is also an entity; let's assume that we name that entity, entity 5; then the diagram can be changed to

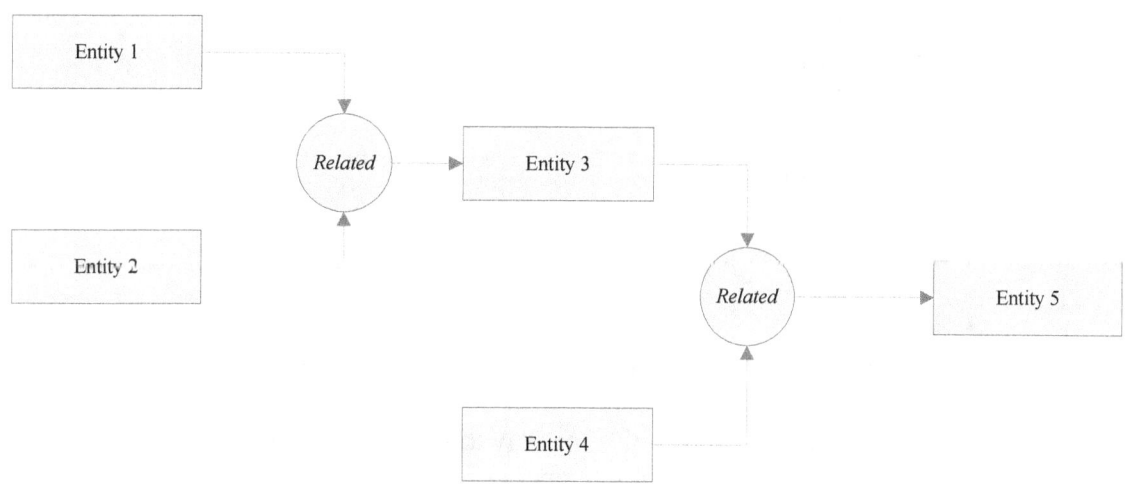

By understanding the relationship entity itself from the diagram above, then the same diagram can be reduced to the form below, where entity 3 is now shown, since it is already taken into consideration in the relationship.

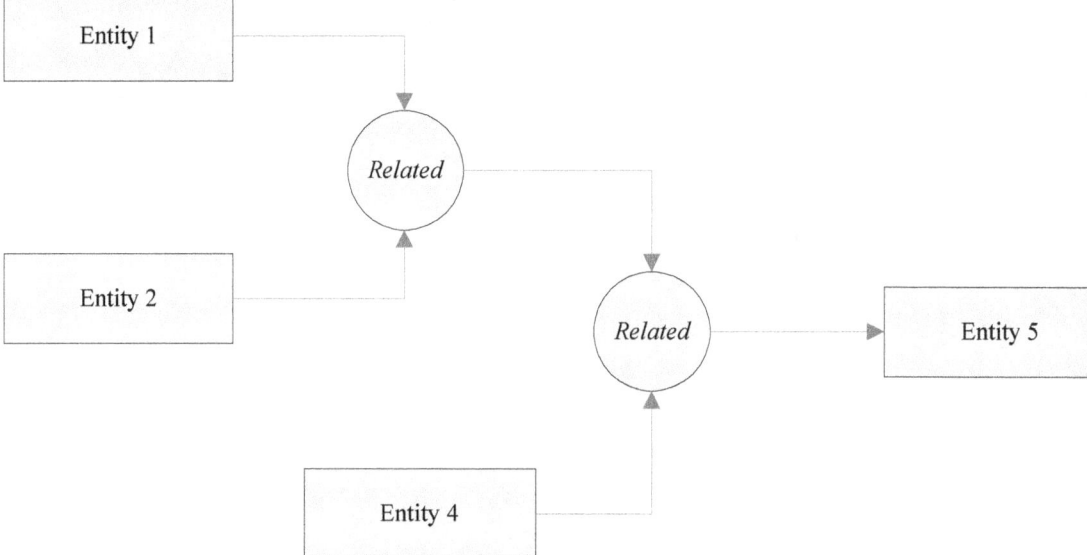

Available Option

Available options for the relationship entity include:

- Relationship
- Relation
- Related
- Any relation name
- Difference
- Similarity
- Comparison, compare etc.
- Attached
- Etc.

While the relationship entity can be used for comparison, nevertheless it is important to know that comparison of entities take understanding of the principle to a higher level. The way to look at it, since in order to compare two entities both of them must be well understood; in this case we simply increase our understanding of those entities. Since the understanding of communication depends on the principle itself, all that we do during the process is increasing our understanding of the principle. In term of comparison, the diagram below shows an example. Assume that entity 3 is the comparison of entity 1 and entity 2.

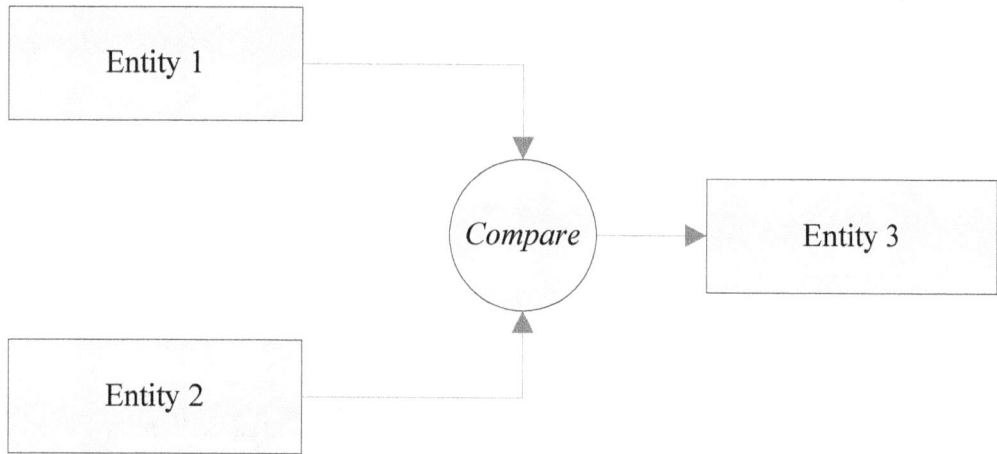

In term of relationship, the first diagram above shows that *entity 1* is related to *entity 3* and *entity 2* is related to *entity 3*. By using the relationship arrow, we can represent them as shown by the two diagrams below.

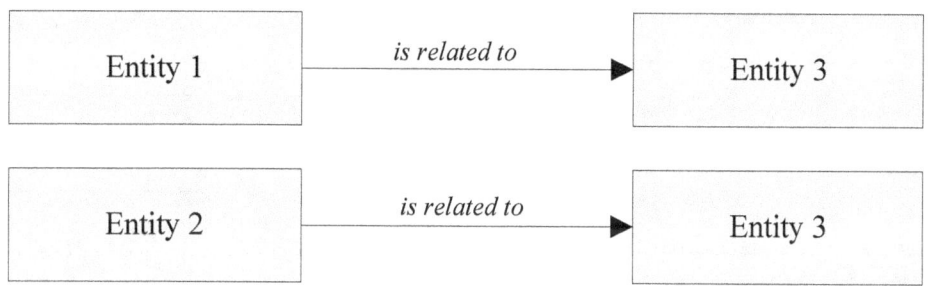

We can use curl braces to annotate the relationship entity. By using curl braces, we can annotate some of the diagrams above in the form below. The first diagram below assumes that *entity 1* and *entity 2* are related, while the second one assumes that *entity 1* and *entity 2* are comparable.

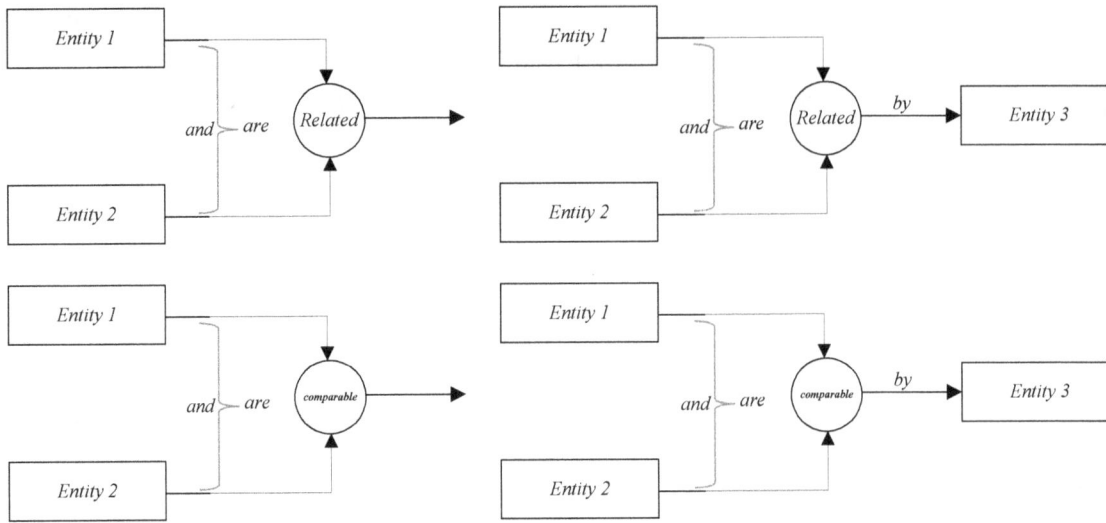

The relationship entity above can also be used as an attached entity to show an entity that is attached to another entity. Assume that *Entity 1* is attached to *Entity 2* by *Entity 3*, then we can use the relationship entity with the attach option to show that. In this case, the relationship entity is used as an *Attached* entity as shown below.

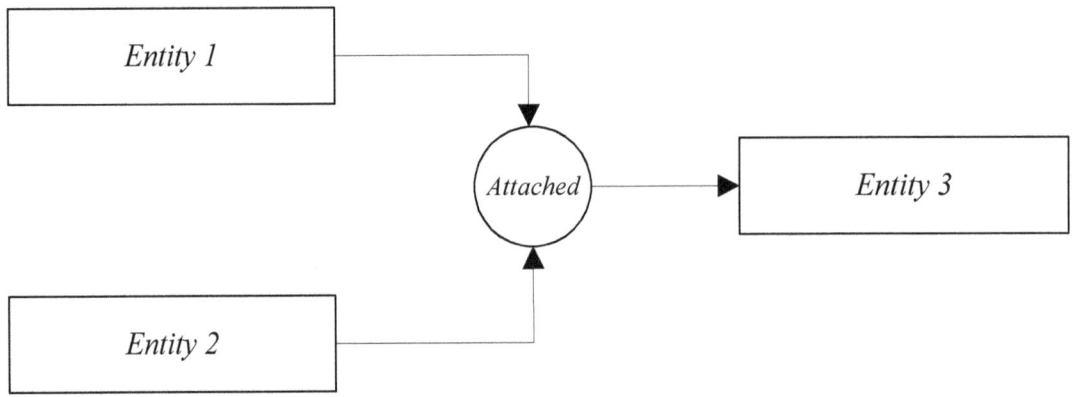

Since we use the principle entity to validate other entities, the relationship entity can be used in conjunction with the principle entity to show the relationship between that entity and the principle entity as shown by the diagram below. Assume that *Entity One* is related to a given principle, and then the relationship entity can be used with *Entity One* to relate *Entity One* with the principle entity.

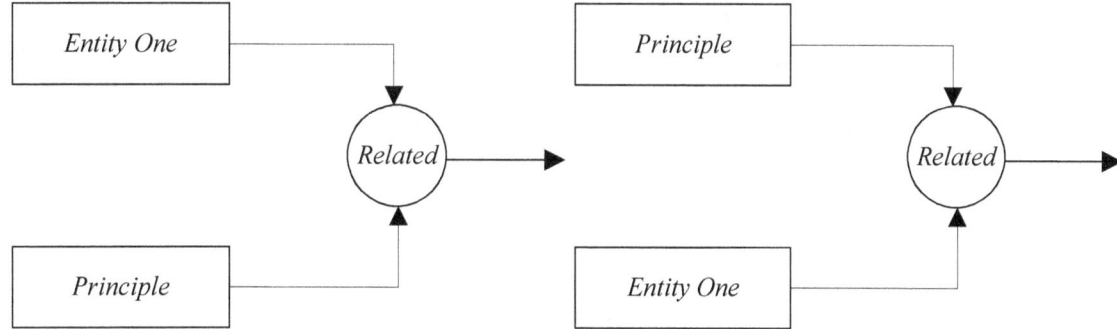

The relationship entity can also be used to relate an entity with the aspect of the principle entity as shown by the diagram below. Assume that *Entity Two* is and entity, where *Aspect One* is an aspect of the principle entity, then if *Entity Two* is related to *Aspect One*, then we can related *Entity Two* to *Aspect One* by using the relationship entity.

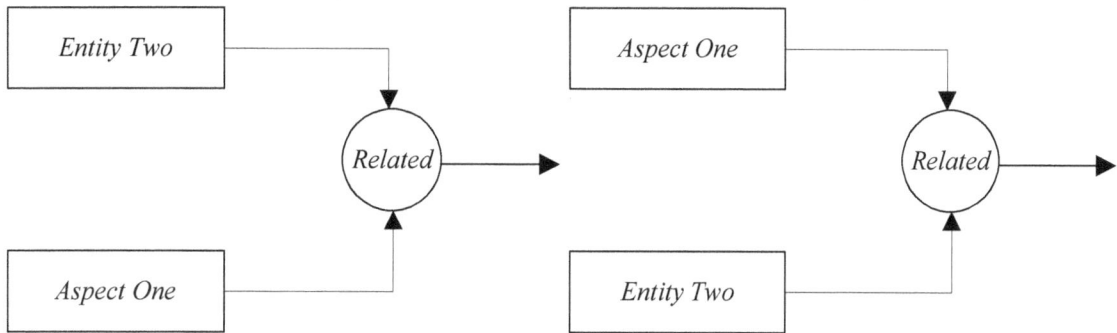

Entity Attach to Other Entity
An entity that is attached to another entity can be show in a form represented by the diagram below. Assume that *Entity 1* is attached to *Entity Two*, and then *Entity 1* and *Entity 2* can be shown by this diagram. The diagram above shows two entities that are attached by another entity, while the one below shows two attached entity. In the diagram above, we

know the attached entity, while we do not know it from the one below.

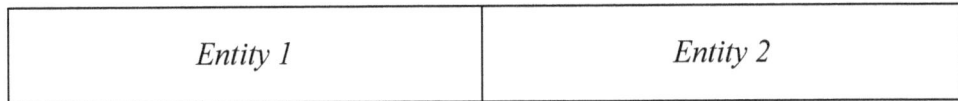

| Entity 1 | Entity 2 |

Identify Multiple Entities as an Entity

In term of entity, since an entity can be composed or included multiple entities, sometime it may be possible for us to show multiple entities as one entity. In this case, we can follow the instruction below to show that. Let's assume that we identify two entities: *Entity One* and *Entity Two*. In this case, it may be possible for us to show those two entities as one entity as shown below.

The two entities above are the entities that we identify. Assume that those two entities are part of another entity, in this case it is possible for us to show them as one entity as shown below.

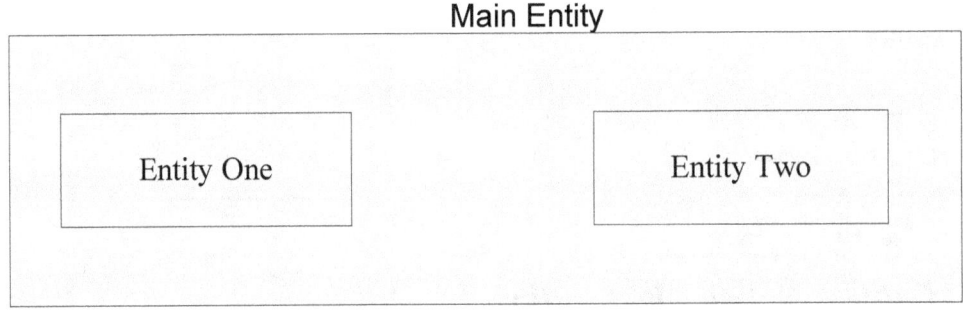

The way to look at it, assume that we have a main entity that makes up *Entity One* and *Entity Two*, in this case we can show both entities as one entity. That makes sense, since the main entity is also an entity, so do the parts of that entity. We can draw an arrow from *Entity One* to *Entity Two;* since the main entity is also an entity, in this case we can show the main entity below without being shown *Entity One* and *Entity Two*. While we call it main entity here, any other name can be used. The way to look at it, we can use the entity element to show entities as one entity.

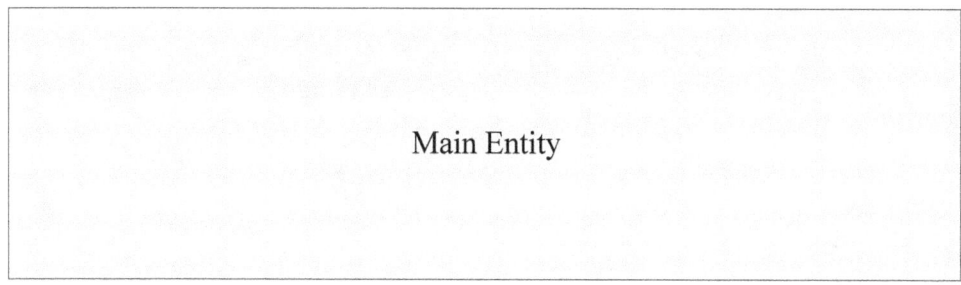

Identify Part of an Entity

Given that a part of an entity is also an entity; given that a section of an entity is also an entity, it is possible for us to use the entity element to show the identification of an entity that is a part of another entity. Assume that from *Entity One*, we identify *Entity Two* and *Entity Three,* where those two entities are part of *Entity One*. In this case, we can show or identify those entities in the form below. In this case, *Entity One* is considered to be the main entity that we identify.

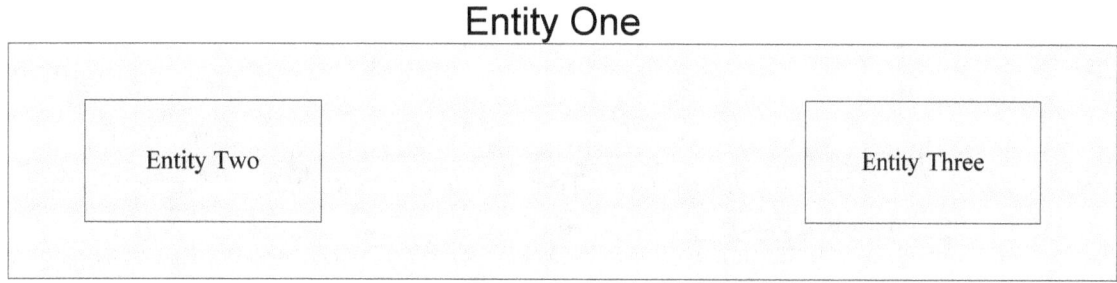

Identify Relationship as an Entity

Since the relationship of an entity is also an entity, in this case it is possible for us to show or identify a given relationship as an entity. To better understand that, let's take a look of the diagram below. Assume that we have a given relationship as presented below.

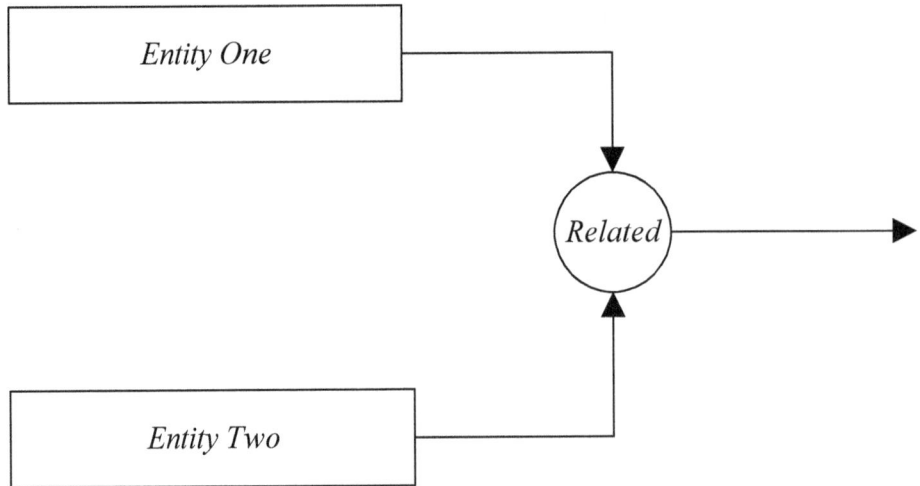

Since the relationship between *Entity One* and *Entity Two* is also an entity, in this case we can show that entity in the form below as an entity.

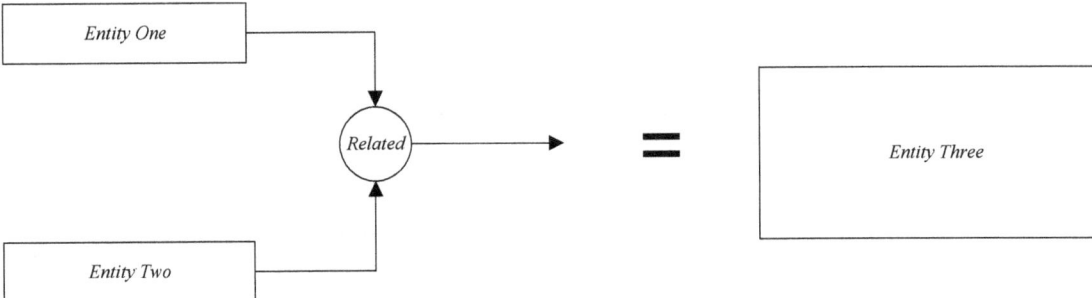

In this case, *Entity Three* is being identified as the whole relationship of *Entity One* and *Entity Two*. To better understand that, we can represent it in the form below.

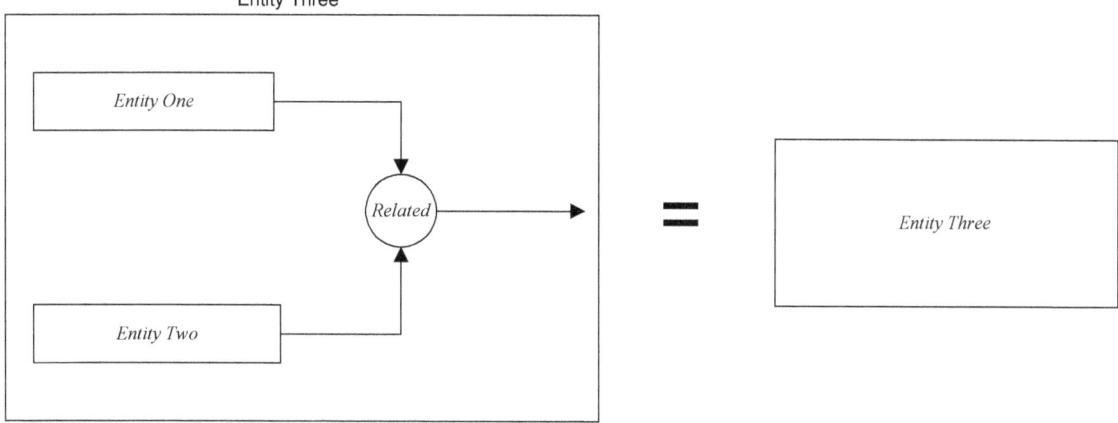

While we show it in the form above, since there is no limit in term of number in a relationship, there is no limit as well in term of number of relationship that can be identified as an entity. Any relationship disregard any number can be identified as an entity.

From the diagram above, the relationship entity inside the dashed area is being used for illustration only. While the relationship of an entity is an entity, it is always good for us not to show a relationship inside an entity. Since the relationship of an entity is also an entity, once we identify that entity, it is always better for us to show that entity as part of the main entity, rather than showing the relationship inside the main entity.

The way to look at it, while we can identify a relationship inside an entity, but we cannot show a relationship inside an entity; since that relationship is being viewed as an entity, it is better for us to show it as an entity. If we were going to show that entity as a relationship, inside another entity, that will further increase the complexity of our model and we will also loose our objective or focus. Our objective is to reduce complexity to help us understand and solve problems not to increase complexity. Keep in mind that does not exist on a piece of paper or a computer screen.

The Location Entity

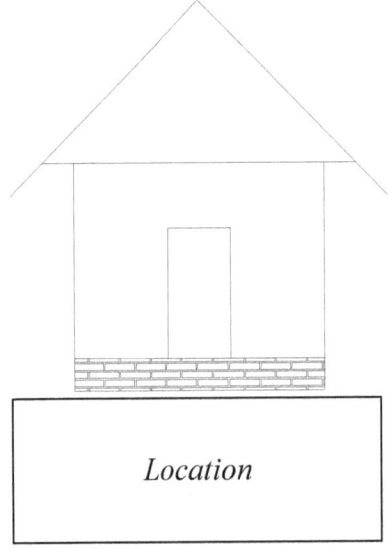

Location

Usage and Description

The location entity can be used to identify a location or a site of operation. Given that the functions that we execute do not take locations into consideration, while we can use the location entity to identify a location, nevertheless it is not necessary for us in the modeling of our application. Since our application does not take location into consideration, it may not be necessary for us to use the location entity to model our application.

While the modeling of our application does not take location into consideration and should not take location into consideration, nevertheless if there is a need to identify the location or the site that we operate within our application, the location entity can be used to identify that site or location. For more information about using the location entity, refer to the example section.

Available Option

Available options for the location entity include:

- Location
- Site
- Location with index or number
- Site with index or number

- Location of operation
- Site of operation
- Etc.

The Area Entity

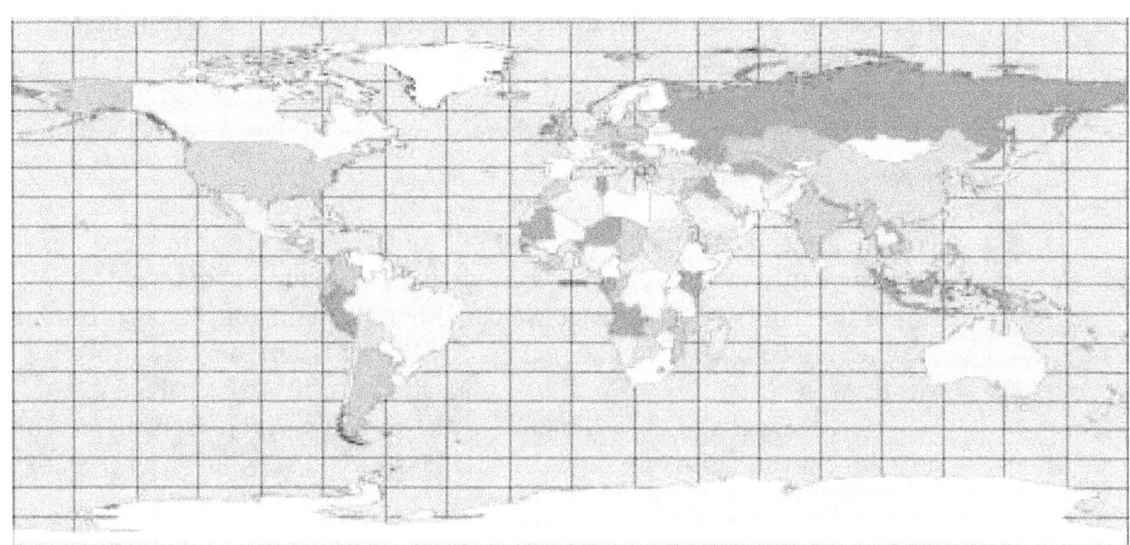

Area

Usage and Description
We can use the area entity to show our area of our operation. Let's
assume that we operate in specific country or area, then we can use the

area entity to identify that country as our area of operation. The area entity can also be used with the site of operation entity to show both our site and our location of operation. For more information about using the area entity and the site entity together with the location entity, refer to the example section. By understanding entity and parts of entity, the area entity can be viewed in the form below as a main entity.

Each area or country in the main entity can be viewed as a part of that entity. For instance, if we identify *Country One*, then *Country One* is viewed as a part of the main entity or simply as an entity within the main entity. In this case, we can label them as parts of the main entity as shown below.

To better understand the area entity, it is always good for us to view it as the main entity. In this case, we can view each area in the main entity as part of that entity. For instance we can think the main entity in the form of the diagram below, where the main entity has parts. In this case, if we identify *Part One*, *Part Two*, *Part Three* and so forth. those parts are considered as parts of the main entity, where each part represent an area of he main entity. This is the same as saying the main area has *Area One, Area Two, Area Three* etc.

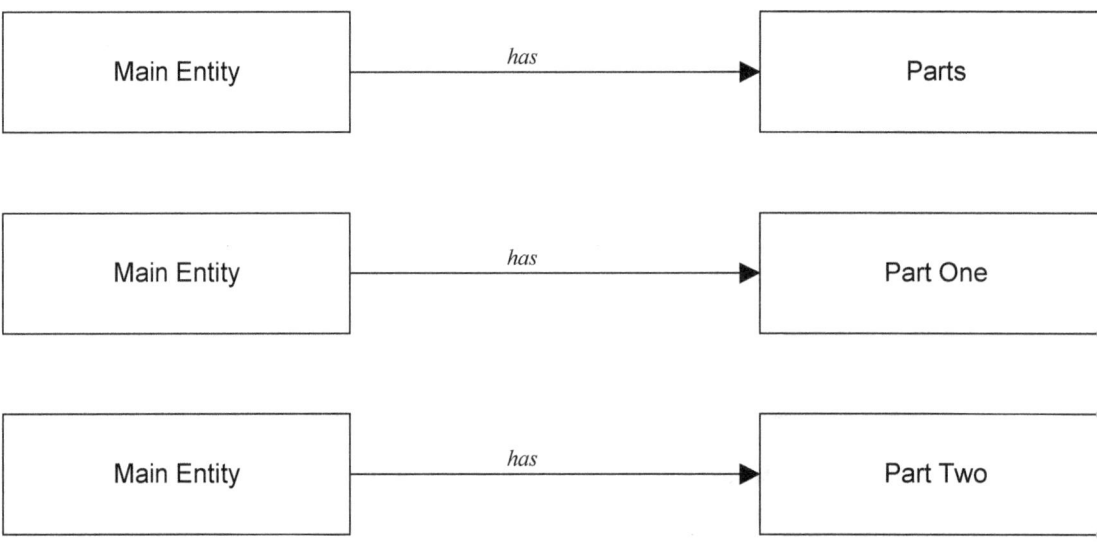

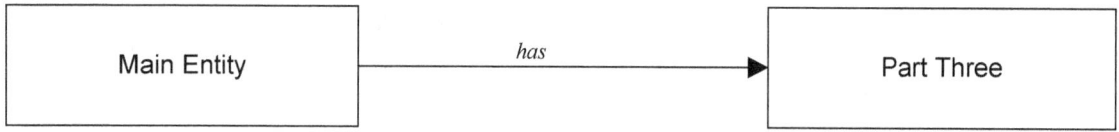

As we said above, the main area includes areas, where those areas are considered to be areas of the main entity. For instance if we identify *Area One*, *Area Two*, and *Area Three*, those areas are considered to be parts of the main entity. In this case, we have

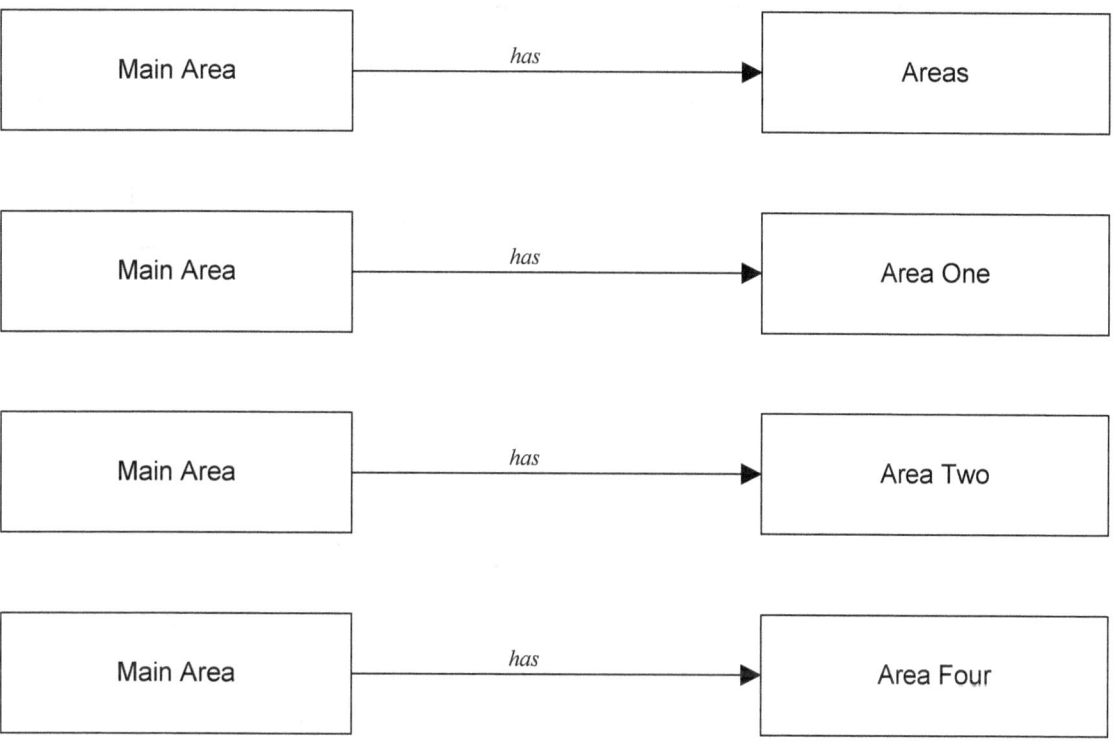

By understanding the explanation and the diagrams above, we can represent the main entity in the form where we can show the main entity and the parts of the entities that include inside that entity. In this case, we have

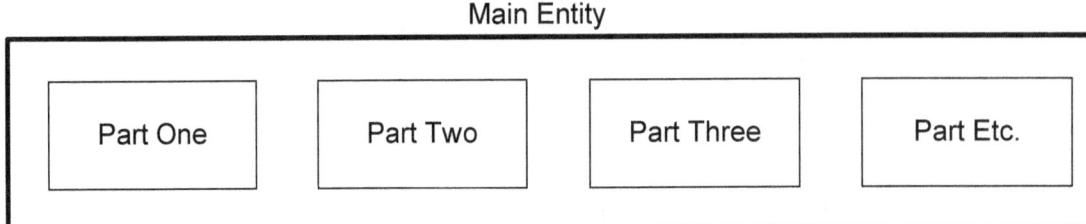

From the diagram above, each part of the main entity is considered to be an area, a country, a location etc. The diagram below represents the main area and the areas that include inside the main area.

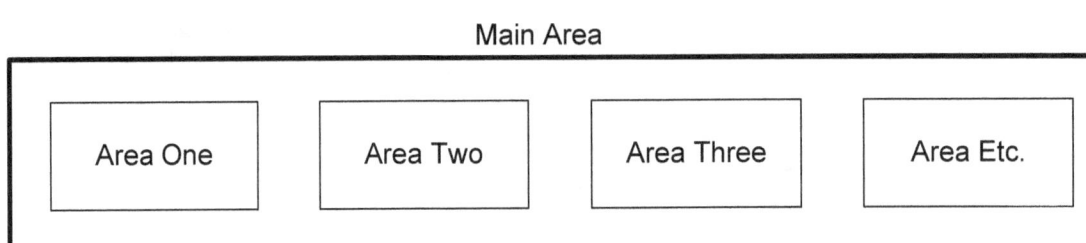

From the diagram above, if we identify the name of an area or the name of a part of that entity, we can also show that in the main entity in the form below. In this case, *Name 1*, *Name 2*, and *Name 3* are viewed as the name of each part of entity that we identify in the main entity.

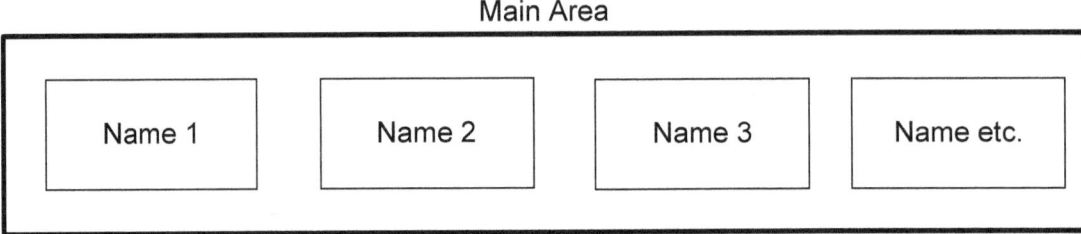

Although that may not be important, but if we want to, it may be possible to show the names of countries or the image or sketch area represented by countries

| Country One | Country Two | Country Three | Country Etc. |

The diagram below show the sketch of each area or country represented in the main area entity.

Main Area

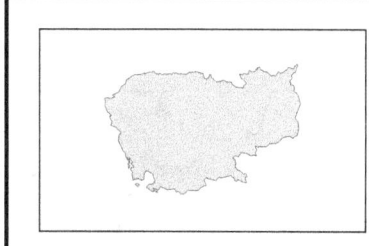 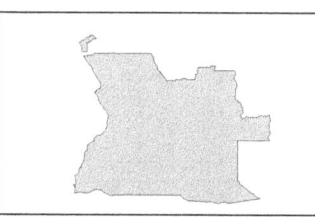 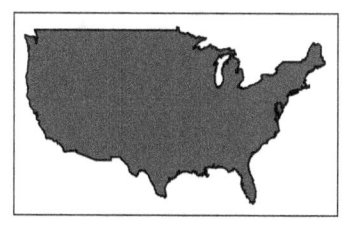

In the diagram below, we represent the countries as *Country 1*, *Country 2*, and *Country 3*. We can also use the name of the countries to represent each area that makes up the main area entity.

Main Area

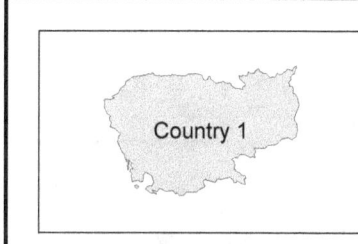 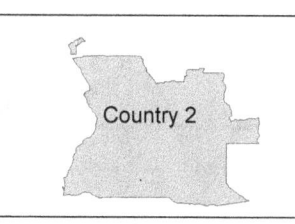 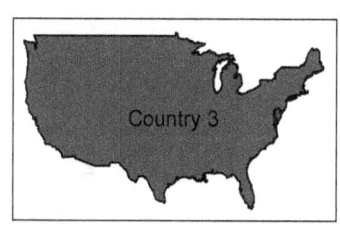

Below, we label them as *Area 1*, *Area 2*, and *Area 3*

Main Area

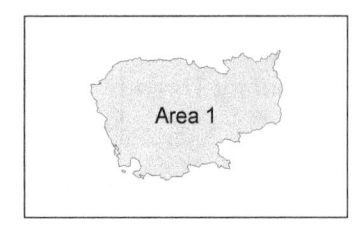
Area 1

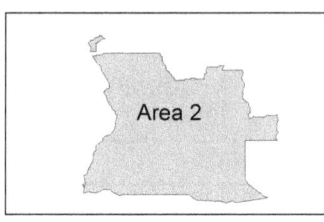
Area 2

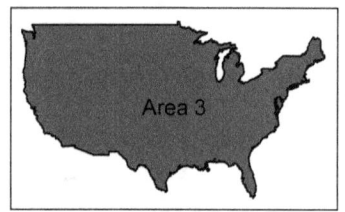
Area 3

Since each area is considered to be a part of the main entity, in the diagram below we label them as *Part 1*, *Part 2*, and *Part 3*.

Main Area

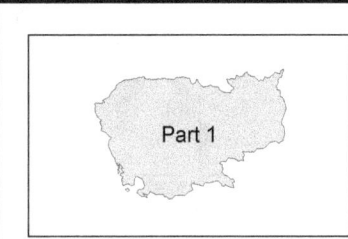
Part 1

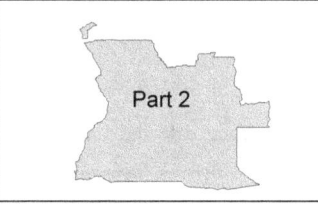
Part 2

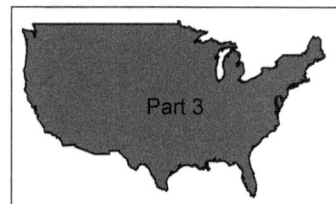
Part 3

The main area can also be used with continuity in the form below. In this case, we use the continuity to show more areas that are not visible in the diagram below.

Main Area

Area 1   Area 2      Area etc.

In term of entity and parts of entity, we can also show the main area entity in the form below, where we can use the *has* relationship label to show an area or a country that is a part of the main entity. In this case we have

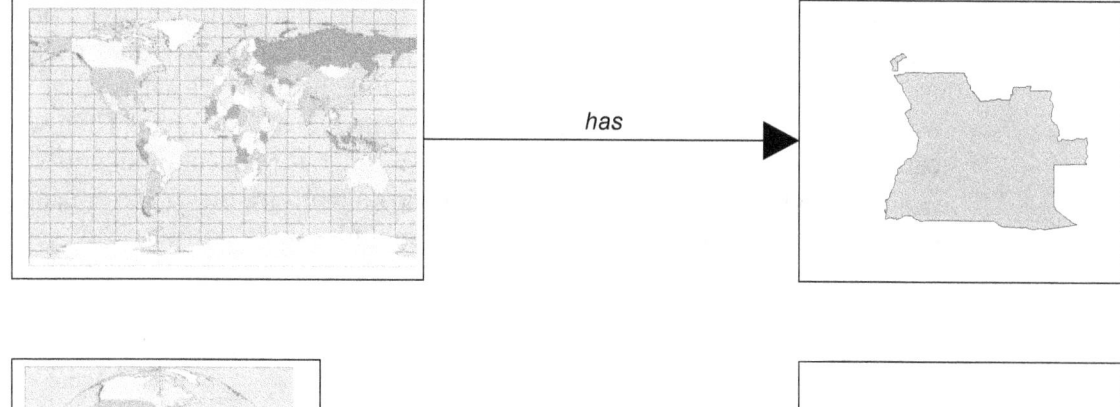

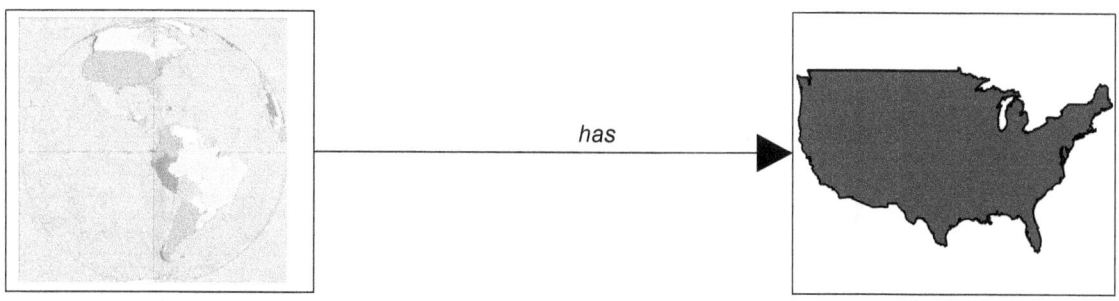

Available Option

Available options for the area entity include:

- Area
- Area of operation
- Area with index or number
- Location
- Location with index or number
- Country
- Country with index or number
- Name with index
- Country name
- State
- City
- City with index or number
- Place
- Etc.

Entity and Aspect of Entity Diagram

Entity and aspect of entity diagram can be shown in the form below. For instance, if we have an entity that has several aspects, then we can use the form below to show that if we want to. Assume that entity 1 has several aspects. In this case, entity 1 has aspect 1, aspect 2, aspect 3, etc. Then we can show that by using the diagrams below. Since the aspect of an entity is also an entity, the diagram to the right shows that. In this case, we use the diagrams below to show an entity that includes other entities.

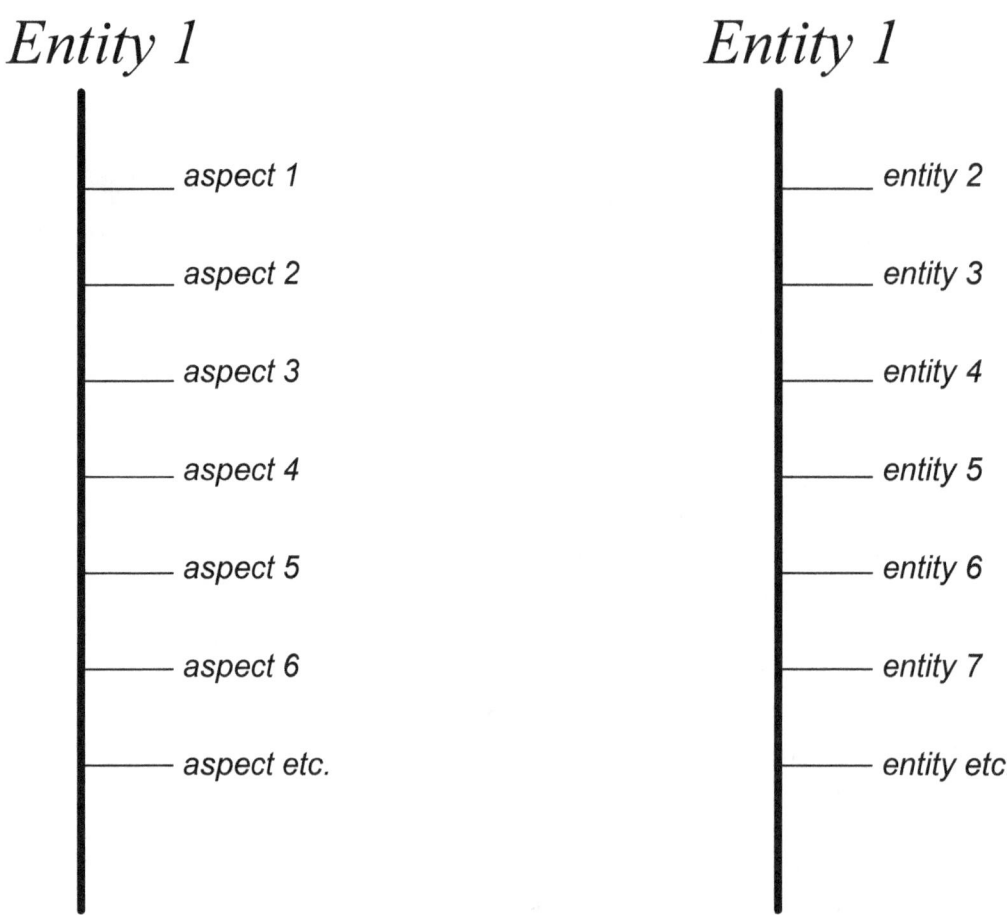

The two diagrams below are the same as the ones above

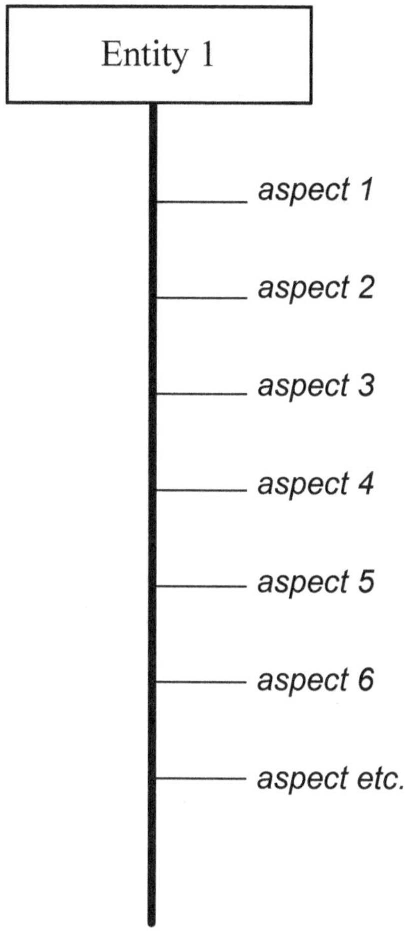

Entity 1
aspect 1
aspect 2
aspect 3
aspect 4
aspect 5
aspect 6
aspect etc.

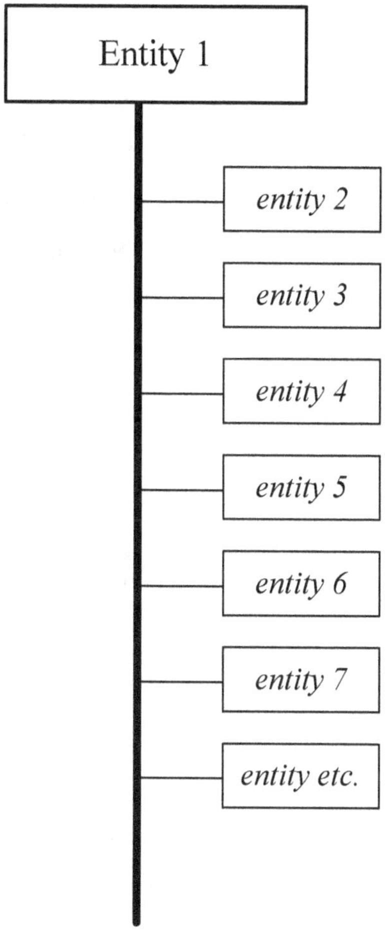

Entity 1
entity 2
entity 3
entity 4
entity 5
entity 6
entity 7
entity etc.

The same diagram above can be shown in the form below. Here we simply use another form to show it. From the diagram below, we only show 4 aspects. The other ones are not listed.

Entity 1
has
aspect 1
aspect 2
aspect 3
aspect etc.

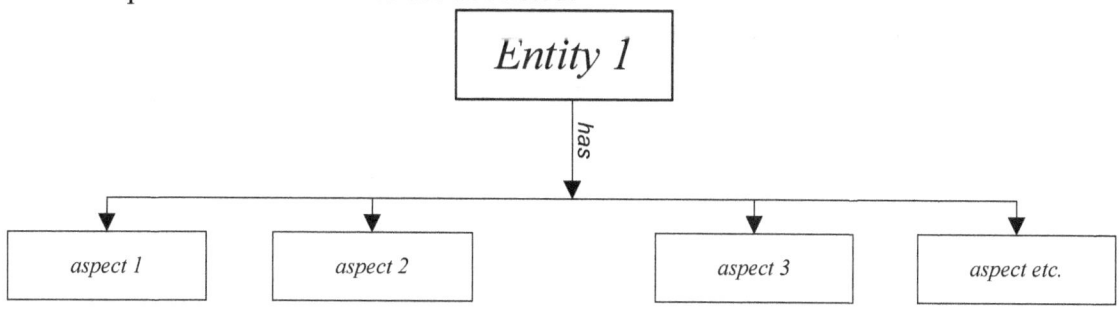

Change of Communication Function from Communication Tabulated Form

Communication	Application Value	Communication Function

Usage and Description

Since our application is communication driven, it makes sense for us to show how any change in our communication affects the application. Since our project is communication enabled, any change in our communication affects the project. By using the table above, we can provide information about how our project change related to communication.

Consider that the overall process as our application, we can also say that the change of our application related to communication. We use the change of communication function from communication table to show how our application execution changes from communication. While the table above shows the basic process, it is always good to expand it to show more information. The following tables can be used to show more information about the change of our application from communication. Keep in mind that, they are the same as the one above, but extend it by providing more information.

Communication	Application Value	Communication Function	Communication Name

Communication Order	Communication Subject	Communication Execution Function	Application Value

Communication Order	Communication Subject	Communication Execution Function	Application Value	Application Name

Communication Order	Application Value	Communication	Application	Communication Function

Communication	Application Value	Communication Function	Communication Name

Communication Order	Communication Date & Time	Communication	Application Value	Communication Function

Communication Order	Communication Date	Communication Time	Comunication	Communication Result

Available Option

Available names for the change of communication function related to communication include

- Change of application related to communication
- Change of application from communication
- Change or communication function related to communication
- Change of communication result related to communication
- Change of communication execution function related to communication
- Change of application function related to communication
- Change of application execution function related to communication
- Change of application result related to communication
- Etc.

Change of Communication Function from Communication Graphical Form

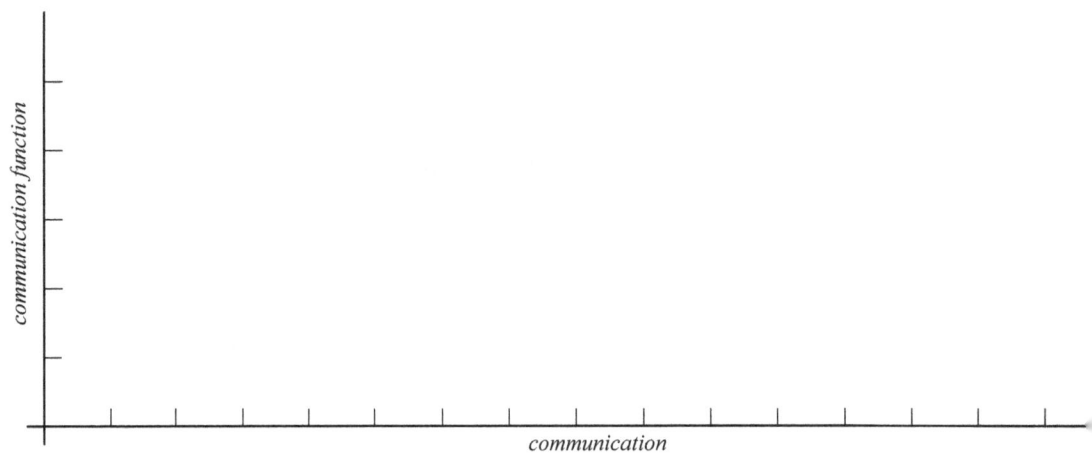

communication

Usage and Description

While we can use a table to show the change of application from communication, we also use the graph above to show or plot how our communication function changes related to our communication. For instance, if we are working in a project and we consider that project as our application, since that project is a function of our communication, we can use the graph above to show how that project changes from our communication. Since we consider that project as our application, we can use the graph above to show how that application changes from communication.

While we can use multiple tables as shown above in the table version to provide more information about the changes, we can also use the graph to show the same information as well. In this case, we can customize the graph axis and the labels to show the information. We use the graph axis above to show or plot the change of the communication function related to communication.

Available Option

Available options name for the graph above include

- Change of communication function
- Change of application
- Change of communication execution function
- Change of application result
- Change of the project
- Etc.

Graph Line and Graph Point

Description and Usage
When using the graphical form to show the change of our application related to communication, we can use the graph line and point with the axis to show the changes. We can rotate the line to any location to reflect the changes. We can also extend the line and add to it when constructing our graph.

Graphical Axis Entity

Description and Usage
Depend on the information we want to show, we can use the graphical axis entity above for that. The graphical axis entity can be used together with graphical lines and points to represent information. Since graphs are considered to be communication entity, then we can use the graphical axis with graphical lines and points as communication elements in term of communication to represent information.

Available Option
Available option for the graph axis entity includes any other name we want to give the axes.

The Continuity Entity

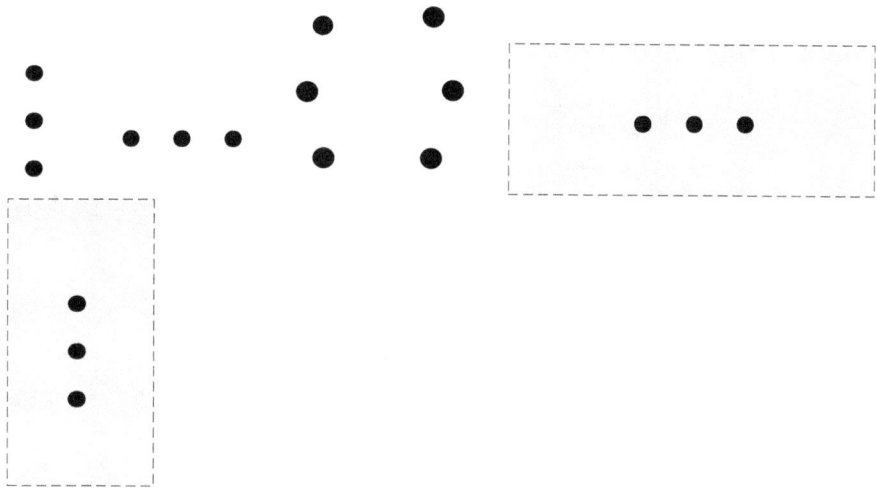

Description and Usage

We can use the continuity entity to show the presence of continuity. For instance if an entity is continue, we can use continuity to show that. For instance in a group of 50 people, we can show 3, and then use continuity at the end for the rest. We can also use continuity in the middle, and then show the last one at the end. Continuity can be used wherever it is needed. Continuity can be used with any entity, whenever it is needed. For instance we can use it for part of communication function, part of application and with all others whenever it is needed. The arc type continuity can be used for the people work together diagram. Refer to the example section for more information about using continuity.

Group of People

Within our project diagram, if space is an issue we can use the following diagrams to show selected group of people, see the example section for more information. Group of people can be shown in the project by using both of the diagrams below. We can use the first diagram to show selected group of people on a computer screen, while the second one is to be used on a piece of paper or a drawing board.

When using the linear form of grouping as shown above, we can also use continuity to show a large group of people for instance. The diagram below shows a group of 50 people. We use continuity to show that there are more people in the group than the ones that are visible to us as shown by the diagram below. We can put the continuity after two or after three it does not matter. The using of the continuity shows there are more people in the group.

By understanding the person entity, the principle entity, and the relationship between the person entity and the principle entity, a group of people can also be identified as shown by the diagram below.

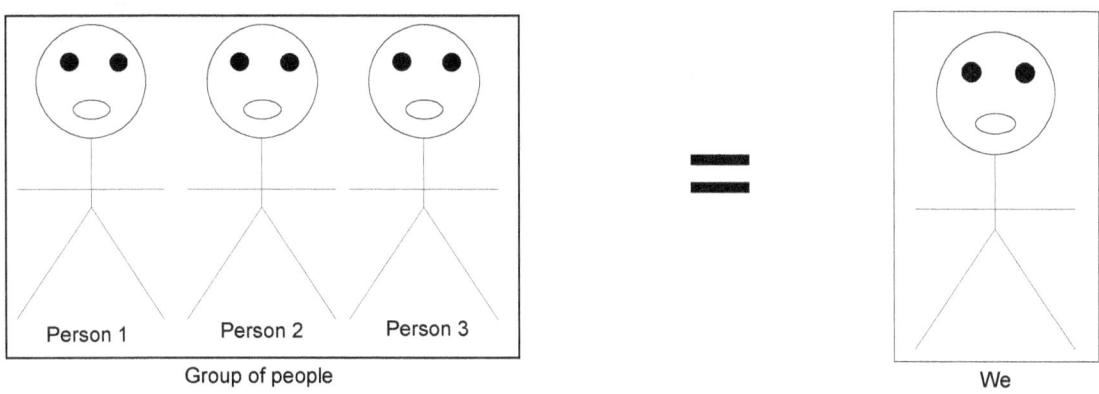

We can represent a group by using the abbreviation G. For instance if we have a group of 3 people in our application, then we can denote the group as G_1 and represent it in the form of

$$G_1 = P_1 + P_2 + P_3$$

By using indexing and summation, for **L** group of people in our application, we can represent them in the form of

$$G = \sum_{l=1}^{L} G_l$$

This is simply a summation of groups in our application. The number of people in group can be varied and each group can be represented with the people as we have shown earlier; refer to the example section for more information.

Sub Application and Part of Application

If the application is segmented into several parts, some parts of the
application can be grouped to give a single part as shown from the
diagrams below. The first diagram shows that the application is divided
into part 1, part 2, and part 3. In the second diagram, we simply use the
empty container to group part 1 and part 2 of the application. To preserve
space, we then use the compressed form of grouping to group part 1 and
part 2, which results to the third diagram.

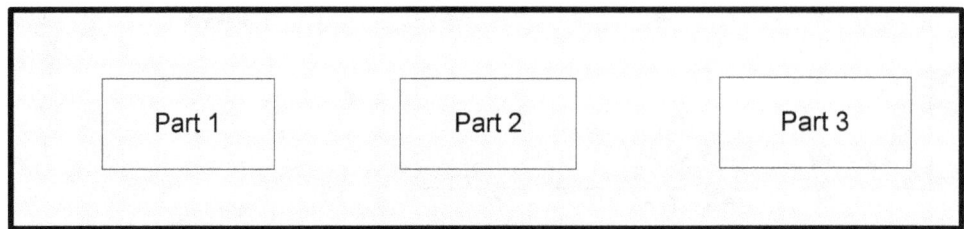

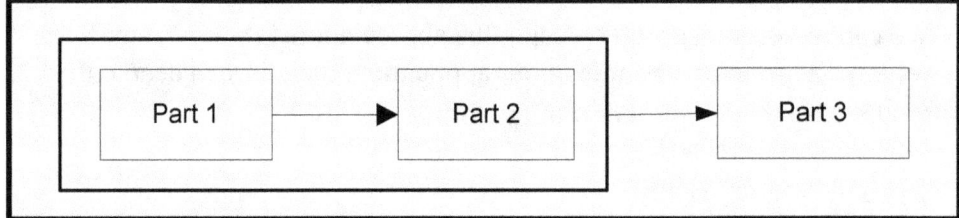

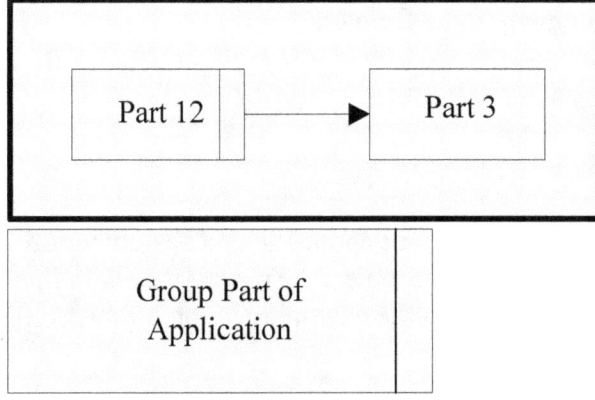

If the project is divided into several sections, it maybe possible to have sub applications on that project; a sub application is considered to be a part of that application that includes other parts. A sub application can also be connected to a sub function. We can also say that the parts of a sub application can be linked to a sub function. The symbol of a sub application is similar to the one of a sub function. The diagram below shows the usage of sub application. From the diagram, we can see that the application is made of two parts, but the first part is considered to be a sub application. The diagram to the right shows the general form of a sub application.

Application

If our application is divided into several parts, then we can represent the parts of our application in the form below. Let's assume that our application is made of 3 parts, in this case we can have

$$A = A_1 + A_2 + A_3$$

By using summation and indexing assume that we have N part of application in our project, then we can have something like

$$A = A_1 + A_2 + A_3 + \cdots + A_N$$

$$A = \sum_{n=1}^{N} A_n$$

Sub Application Result and Part of Application Result

If the project is divided into several sections, it maybe possible for us to use sub application result as well; a sub application result is considered to be a part of the overall result. Assume that our project is made of 5 sections, where each section is managed by a different person and different people work on each section. In this case, the result of the project will be the combined result of the 5 sections. To show that, we can us sub result or part of the result. The first diagram below shows that the application result is made of two parts: part 1 and part 2. The second diagram shows that part 1 of the application result includes other parts inside. In this case, part 1 of the application result is considered to be a sub application result. The identification of a sub application result is shown to the right of the third diagram and it is similar to a sub function. Parts of the application result can also be grouped similarly to parts of function by using empty containers.

Application Result

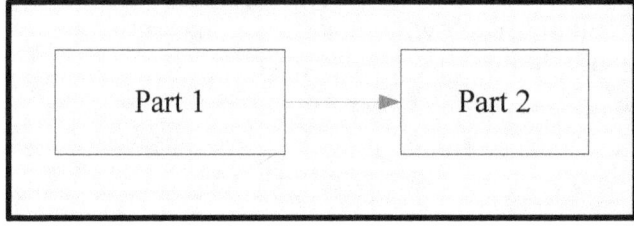

Application Result Part 1

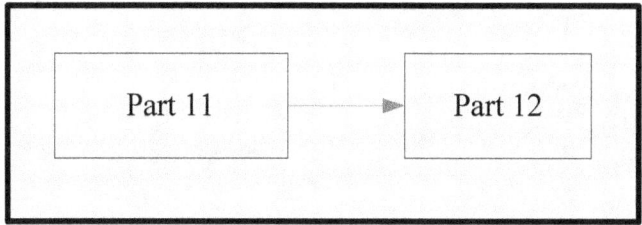

Application Result Part 1

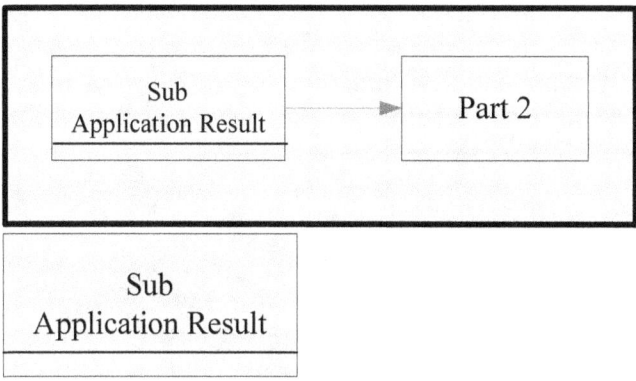

Grouping Part of Communication Function

Since the overall project is driven by our communication, when managed by different people, if makes sense for the communication function to be divided into several sections. We have already seen that from the usage of the empty container entity. The diagram below shows that our communication function is made of three functions.

Communication Function

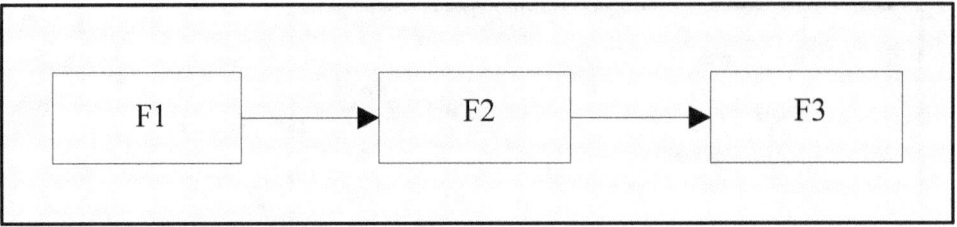

By using the empty container entity, we can group the first two functions of the communication function and leave the last one ungrouped as shown below.

Communication Function

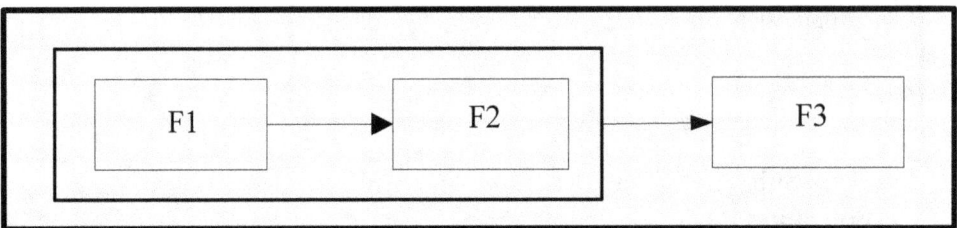

To reduce spacing, we then use the compressed form to group the two functions from the main communication function as shown here. The diagram to the right represents the compressed form of grouping parts of function. F12 is the combined grouping for function F1 and function F2.

Communication Function

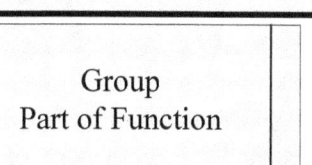

```
┌──────────────────────┐
│ F12      │  →  │ F3    │
```

| Group |
| Part of Function |

Review of Grouping

In this section, let's review what we have learned about sub function, sub application, sub result, part of function, part of application and part of result. We use sub functions, sub applications, and sub results to link to other sections of our project. That usually happens when our project is divided into several sections. The diagram below shows the representation of sub function, sub application, and sub result.

| Sub Function |
| Sub Application |

| Sub Application Result |

Since our project is communication driven, it is important to assign individual function to employees or groups. When that happens, each function is considered as a part of the main function. We can group several parts of those functions into one function. We can also do the same process for application and application result. Below shows the representation of grouping parts of the application, parts of communication function, and parts of communication result in compressed form.

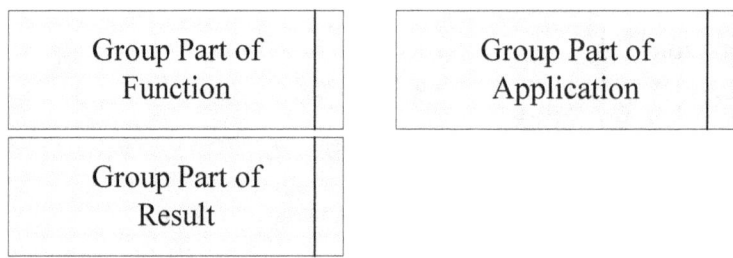

Grouping Communication Holder

Communication holder and external communication holder can also be grouped in the following form. Refer to the example section for more information. The shadow form can be used on a computer if necessary.

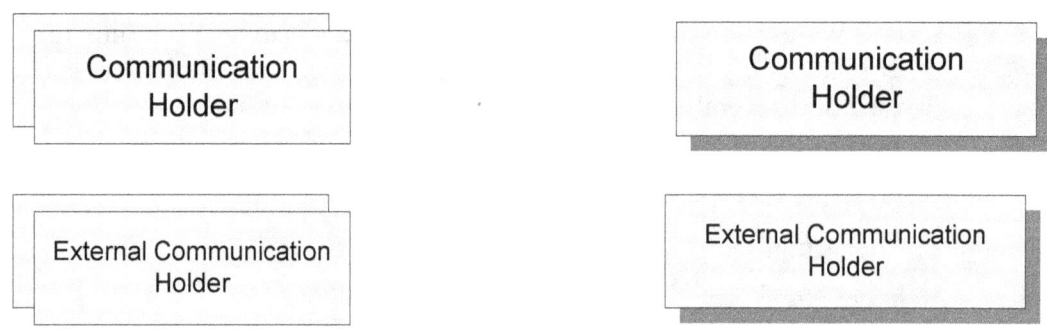

Grouping Entity and Communication Entity

Entities and communication entities can also be grouped in the following form. Refer to the example section for more information about grouping entity.

Grouping Error and Compensator

Similarly to grouping entity above, error and compensator can also be grouped in the following form

Grouping of Problem

As an entity itself, many problems can also be grouped in the following form

Grouping of Feedback

If needed, feedback can be grouped as shown by the diagram below. Assume that there is a need in a project to show all applicable feedbacks, and then the feedbacks received can be grouped on the form below. Refer to the example section for more information.

Feedback

Feedback

Grouping of Analysis

If there is a need in the project to show the list of analysis, then the analyses can be grouped in the form as shown below, see the entity usage sedition for more info.

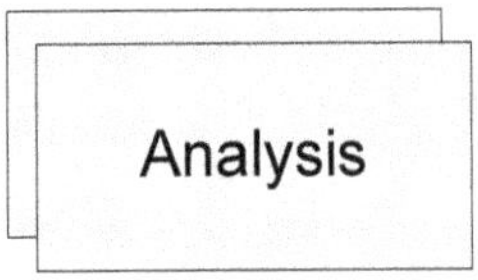

Analysis

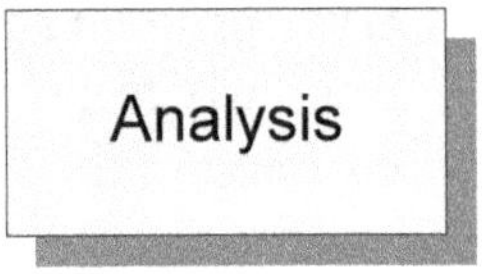

Analysis

Grouping of Question and Answer

While it may not be necessary, however if there is a need to show a group of question and a group of answer, we can group questions and answers in the form below.

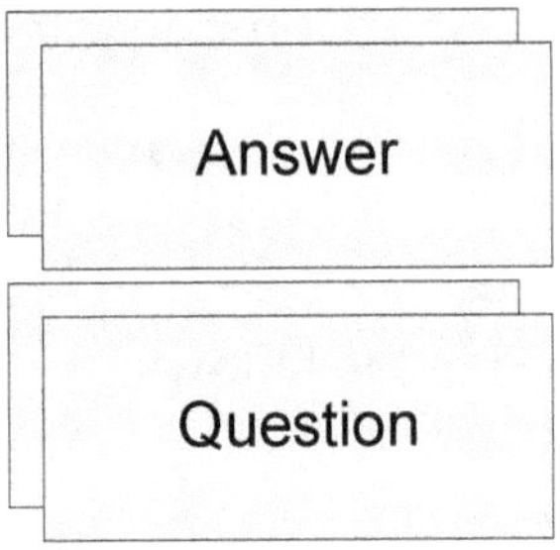

Answer

Question

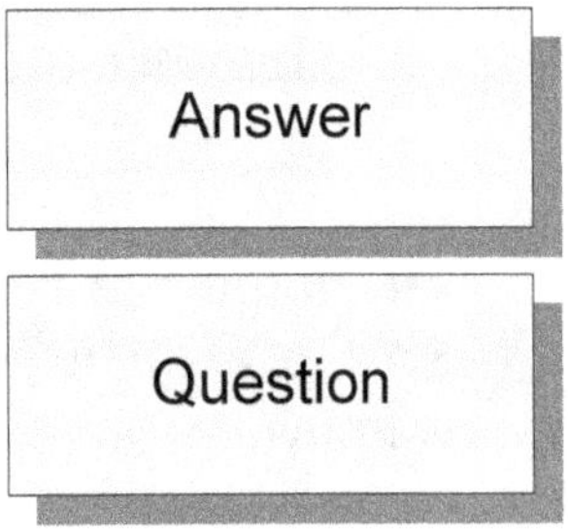

Answer

Question

Some Entities Connection Examples

This section provides some examples of the usage of the entities. We can use this section to learn how to connect some of the entities in an actual project.

Example Number 1
Below we show the usage of the error correction function. In this case, the person to the left can be considered as the children while the one in the right as the parent.

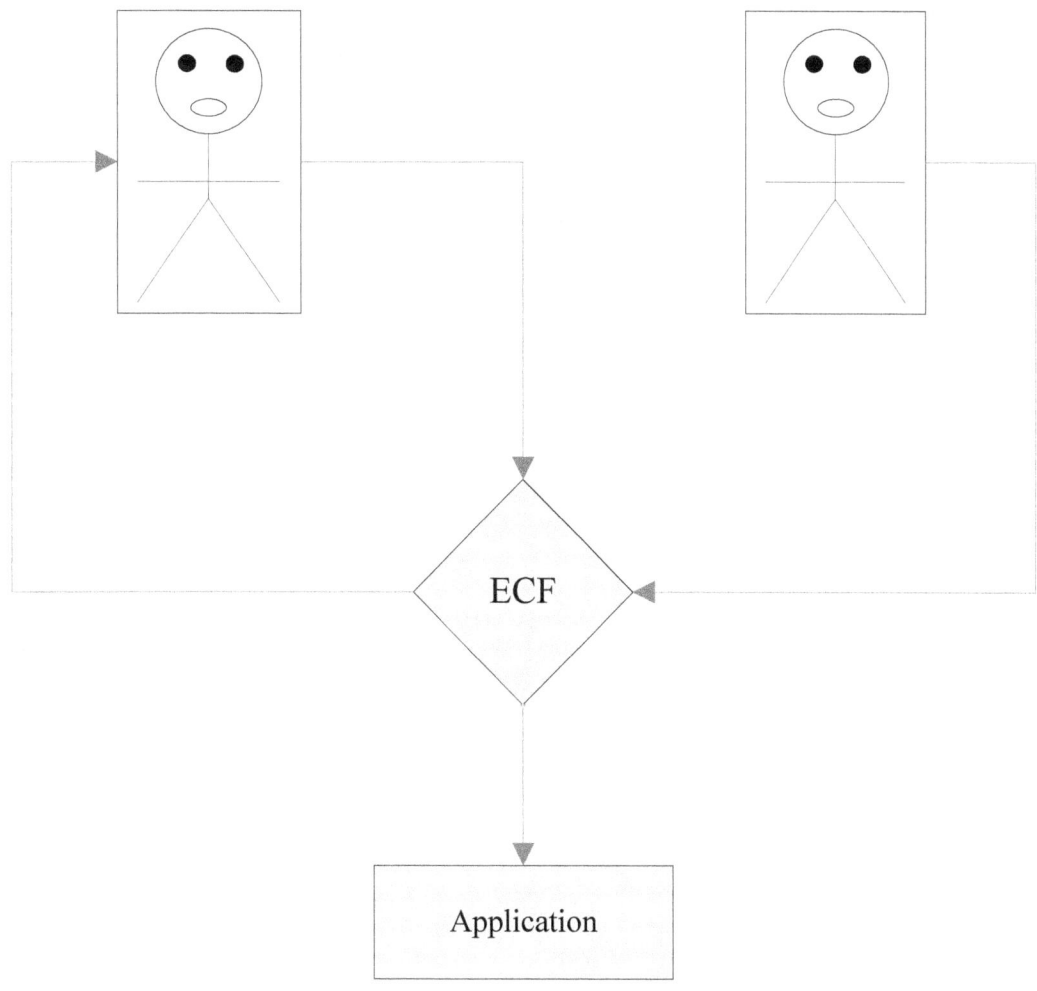

Example Number 2
Since the principle is considered to be the parent itself, then the principle can replace the parent on the diagram above. The diagram below is the same as the one in the example above, except the parent is simply replaced by the principle.

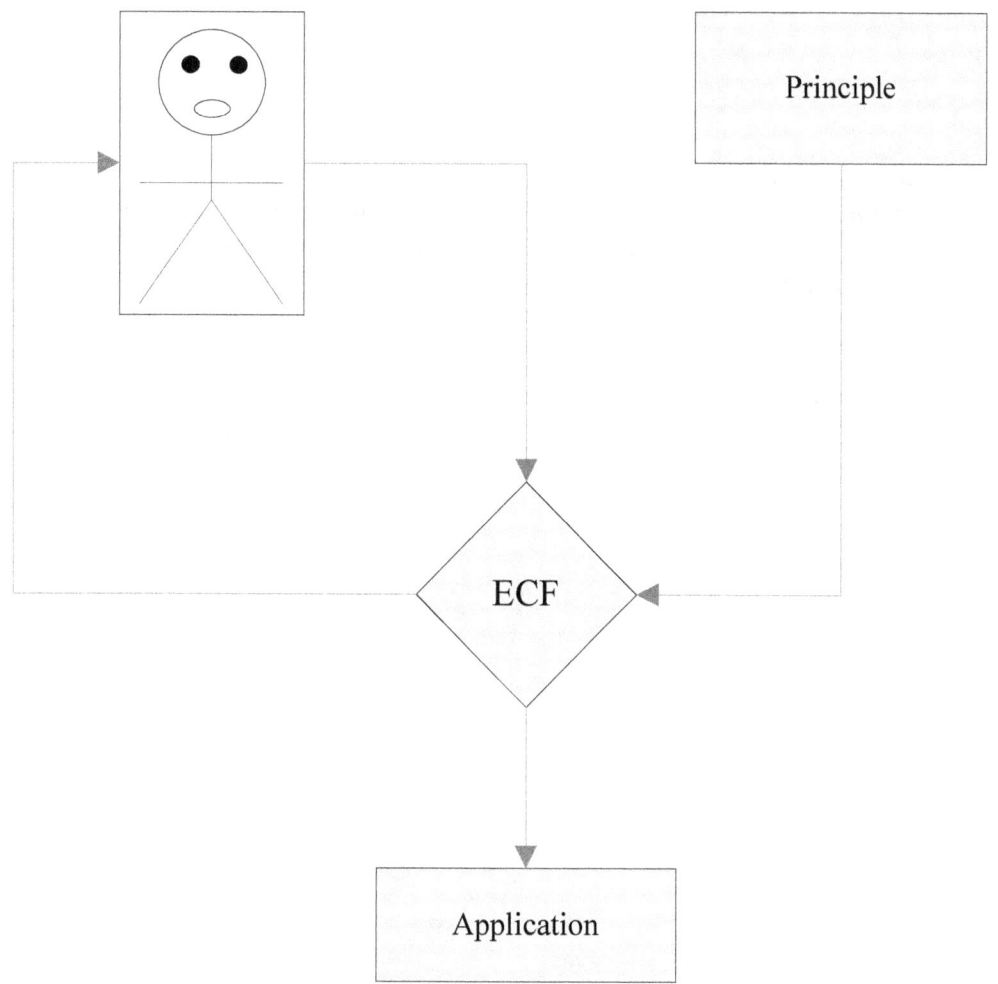

Example Number 3
The diagram below shows the usage of the communication mixture entity. As we know, the communication mixture can take several communications as input. The output of the communication mixture then feeds the communication application mixture as shown to the right. The way to look at it, communications from many people can be connected to the communication mixture entity. In this case, the output of the communication mixture entity contains communications of those people. On the diagram below, communication from four people are connected directly to the communication mixture entity.

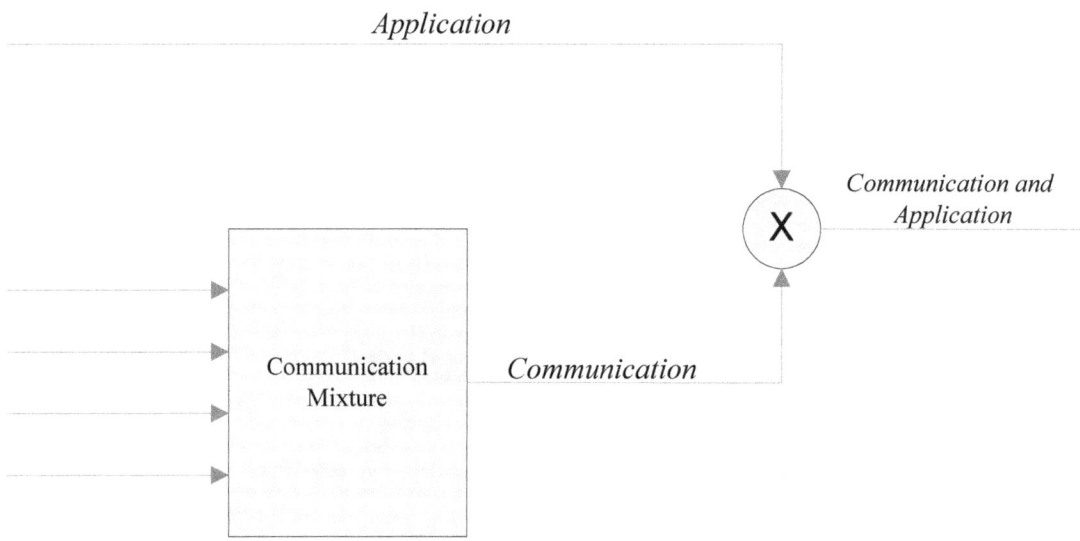

The diagram below is the same as the one above, except the **X** inside the circle is replaced by Mix. Below we use the *Mix* to denote the mixture of the communication and the application. It does not matter; we can simply use the whole word or the phrase.

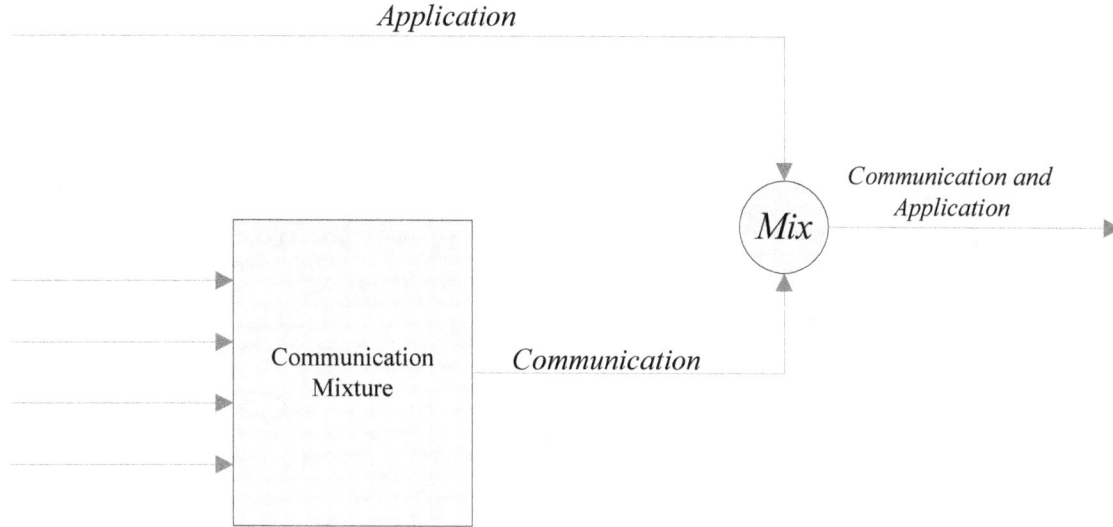

Here we use the short abbreviation to show the mixture of the communication and application. Rather than using the long word, we can use the short abbreviation to show the same thing. The result is the communication function or the execution of the application or execution of the communication function. The diagram is the same as the one above, except the communication is replacing by *x* and the application is replacing by *A* for simplicity

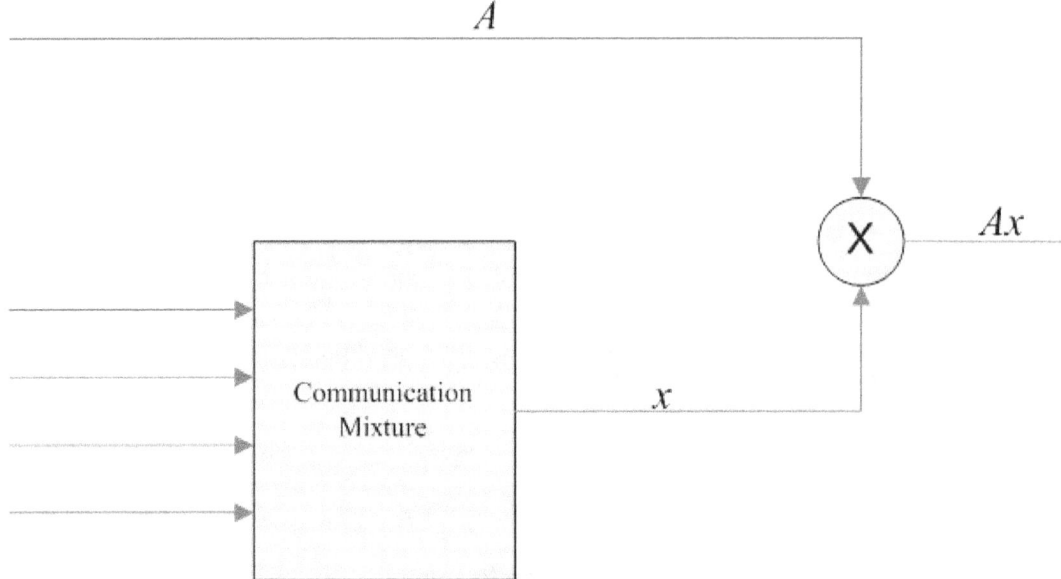

Example Number 5

We do have option to use the communication process entity or the communication mixture with the communication application mixture. It does not matter which one we use, we can still use the communication mixture entity to group our communications. The communication mixture entity can also feed the communication process entity. We can also connect people or communication directly to the communication process entity. The way to look at it, the communication process entity includes inputs for both communication and application. It is always good to group all of our communications as a single entity to feed the communication process entity. The diagram below shows the usage of the communication mixture as a single entity to feed the communication process entity. The communication process entity is the same as **Mix** inside the circle or the **X** insider the circle. The diagram assumes the separation of the application from communication. It is also good to understand that other communication mixture can also feed the communication mixture entity.

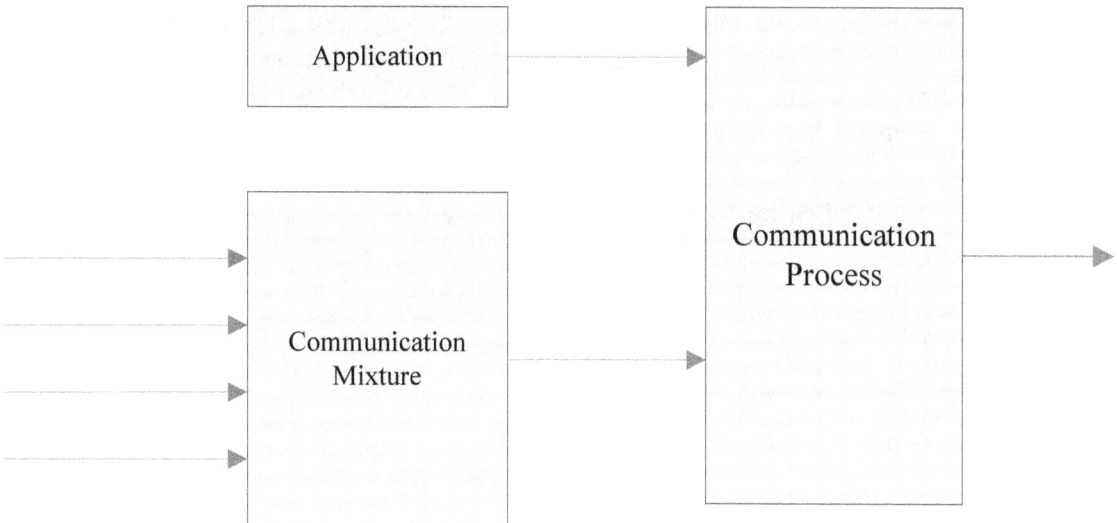

Example Number 6

If the application is divided into several sections, the application entity can be used to show that. Below the application is made of 3 sections, we use parts of application to show that. In this case, each section is considered to be a part of the application. We can also use the grouping entity and the empty container to group part of the application.

Application

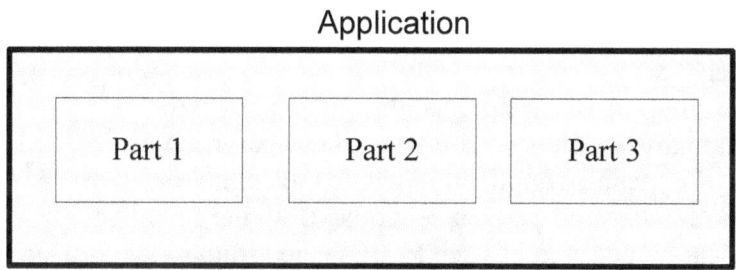

Instead of using the grouping entity as shown above to show the grouping of several parts of the application, the grouping of several parts of the application can also be presented in the following form as shown below. This case depends on the type of paper or drawing board that is being used to model the application. Assume that we are using a portrait size of paper, where we don't have a lot of width to work with, then we case use the portrait form of the application to group the parts of our application. If we want to, we can use arrow to show how the parts are connected together. Below, the diagram to the left is the same as the one to the right, except in the one to the right, we use arrow to show the connection of the parts of the application.

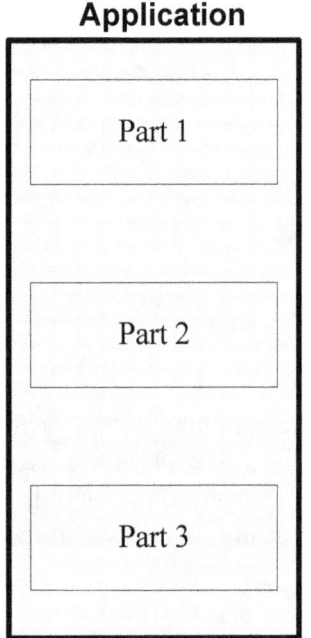 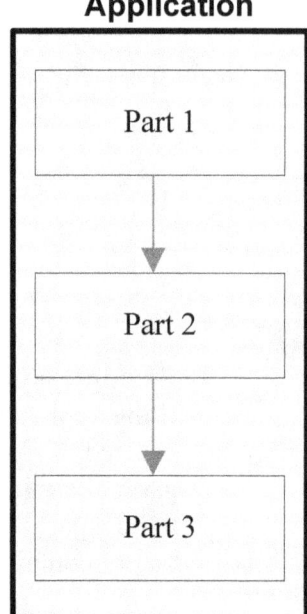

Example Number 7

Comparing to the grouping of the application shown above, for applications that are divided into several parts, those parts can be grouped as shown below. We mean an application where the communication function is divided into several parts or sections. Both the first diagram and the second diagram can also be used to show the grouping of parts of the communication function. The way to look at it, the bigger entity represents the overall communication function, while the small entities represent parts of the communication function. We can also say that the bigger entity represents the overall parts of the communication function. Below, the second diagram is the same as the first one, except in the second diagram, we use arrow to show how those functions connect together.

Communication Function

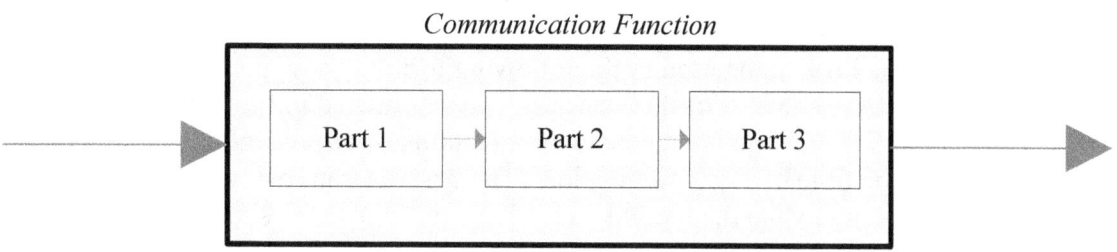

Communication Function

Example Number 8

If the communication function is made of several sections, sub functions can be used to show part of function of the communication as well. Here is an example; in this case F1 is a sub function. This example is similar to the one above, except one of the functions is considered to be a sub function. A sub function is a function that contains other functions inside. If the communication function is divided into several parts, some parts of the communication function can also be considered as sub functions.

Communication Function

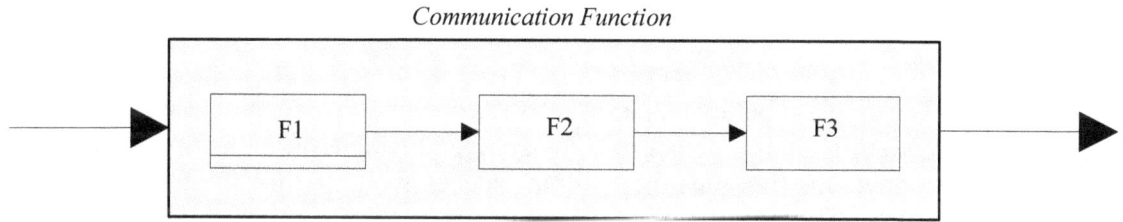

The diagram below shows the expansion of the sub function **F1**. As we have said it, a sub function is a function that contains other functions inside. As shown by the diagram below, we can see that the sub function **F1** above expanded to functions F11, F12, and F13. All those functions are considered to be parts of the main communication function.

F1

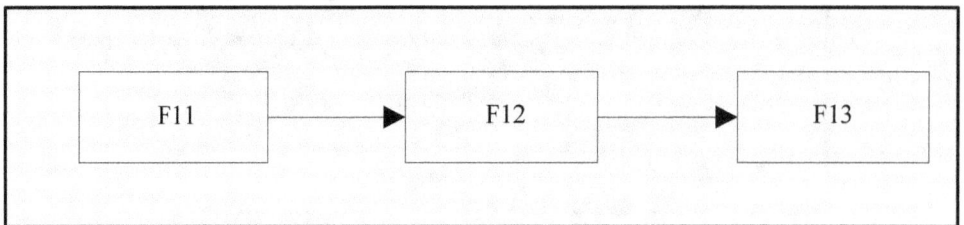

Example Number 9

Time line can be used in the following form to show function execution related to time or to show specific process related to time. For instance, we can use time line to show the execution of our communication function or the time of a communication. The first diagram below shows the first time line while the second one to the right shows the successive time line.

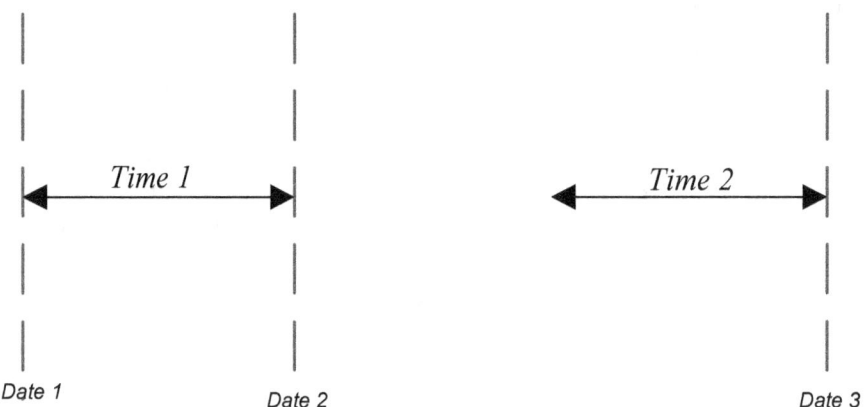

The diagram below is the same as the one above, except that we connect both time lines together to show an overall single time line. All that we do connect the first time line with the successive time line.

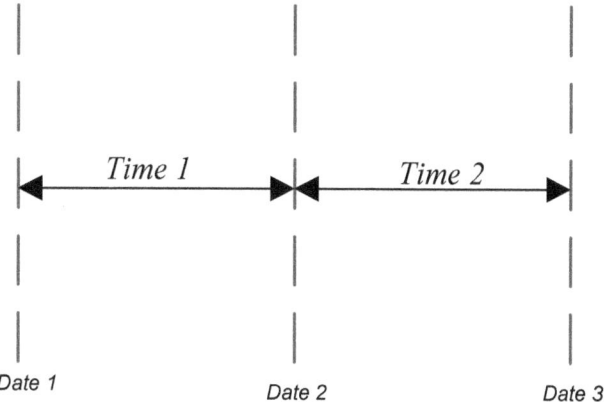

Date 1   Date 2   Date 3

We can also use progress bar with time line to show the progress of our application. In this case, we can use the progress bar with specific time line to show the progress of the application at a particular time. The diagram below uses both progress bar and time line to show the application progress at a given time. In this case we can see at *time 2* we are 15% completed. The diagram to the left is the same as the one to the right, except in the one to the right, the progress of the application is shown at the bottom.

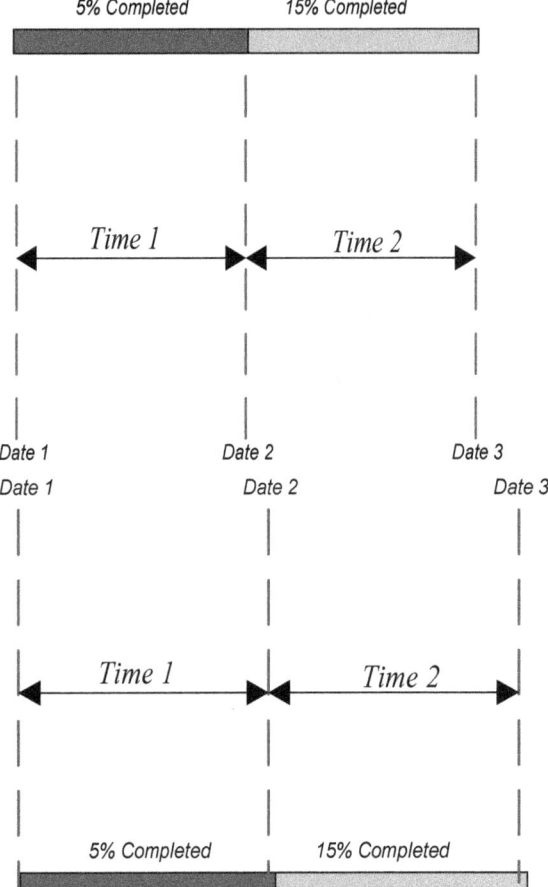

Example Number 10

We know that the communication mixture entity takes communication as input. In this case, we can connect people directly to the communication mixture entity to show how their communications feed that entity. In the diagram below, we connect three people directly to the communication mixture entity. The output of that entity is the total communications of those people.

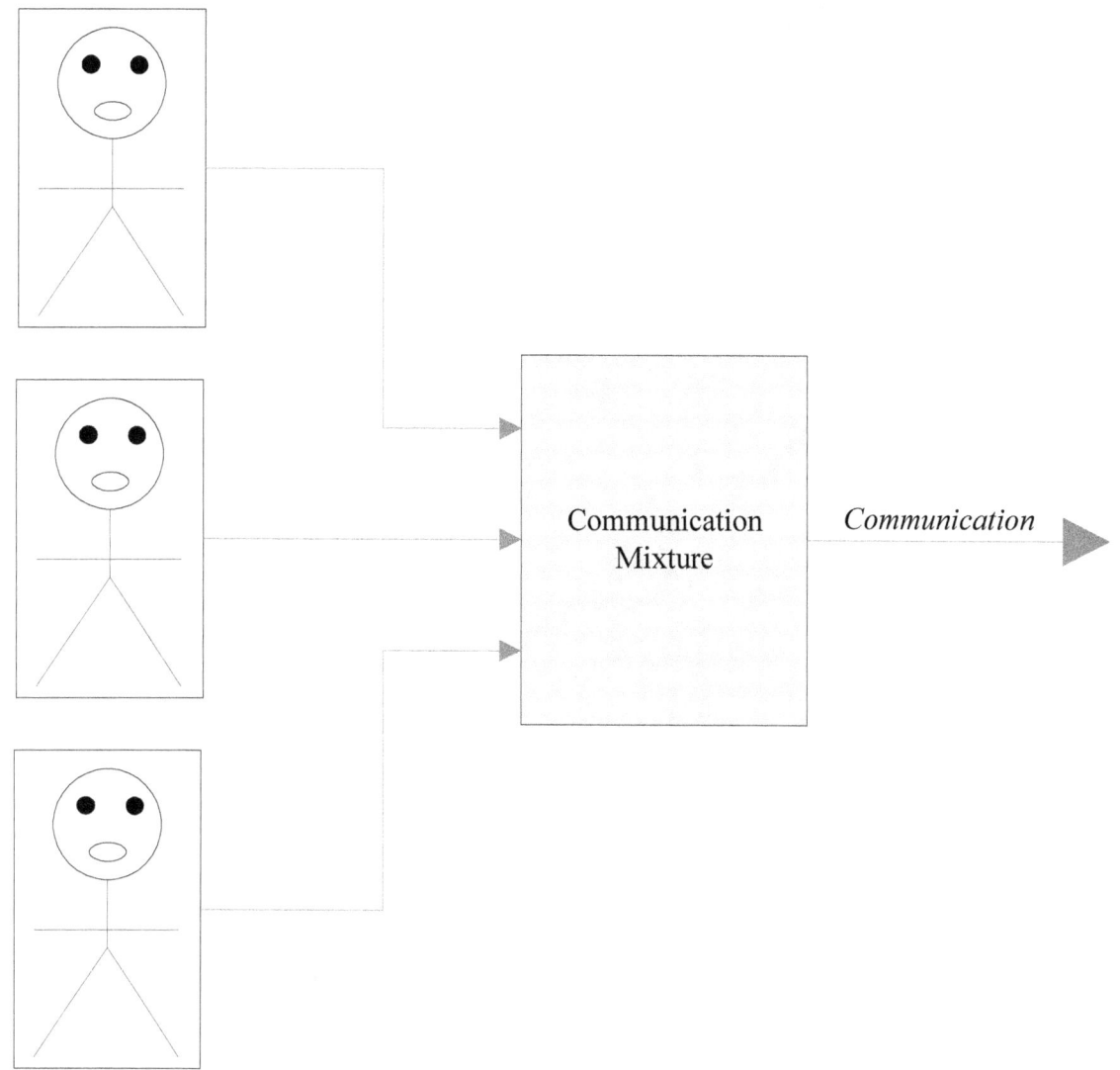

The diagram above can also be represented in the form below

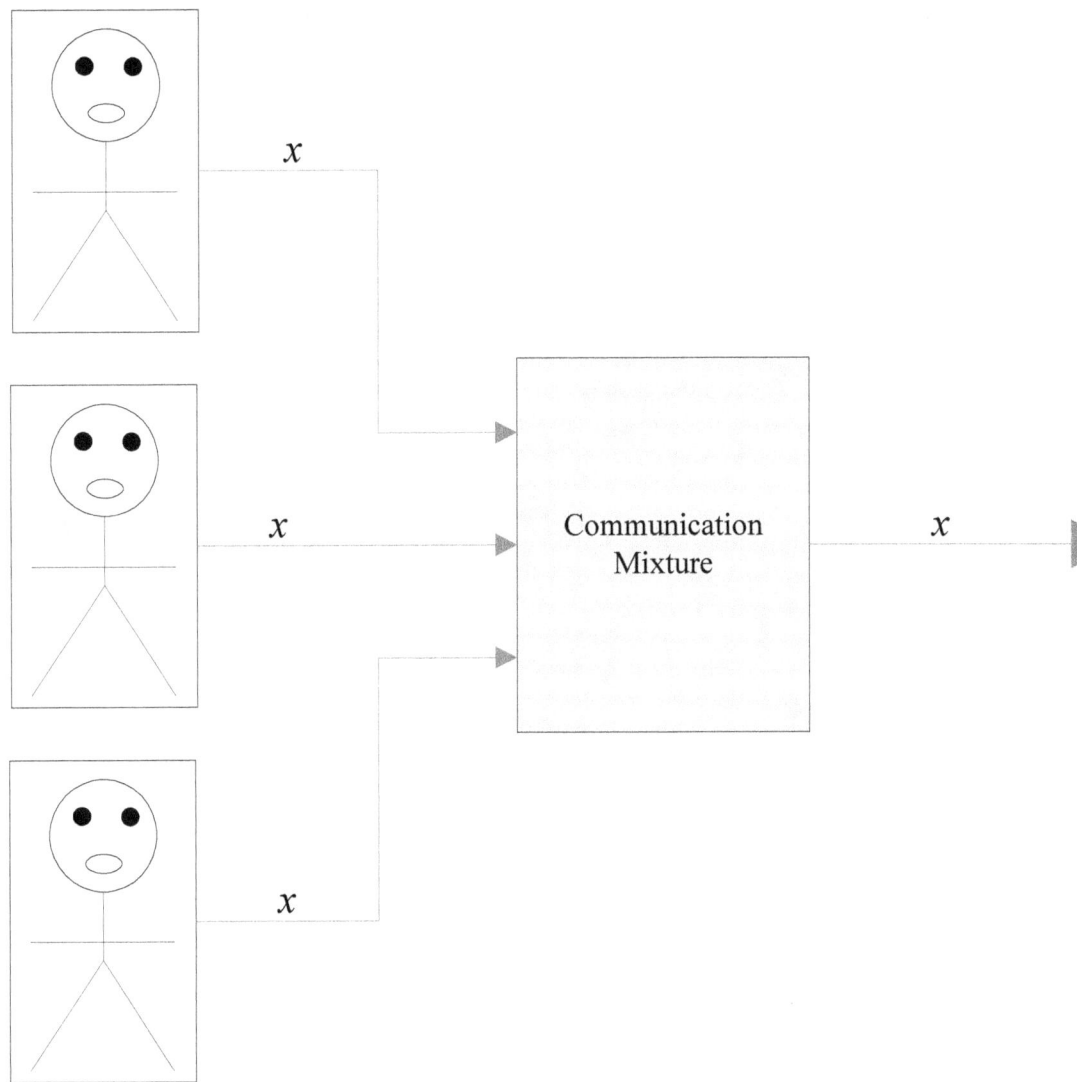

The diagram below is similar to the one above, except the grouping entity is used to show a group of two people. We know that we can use the grouping entity to group people; we can also use it to group communication mixture if we want to, although not necessary. The way to look at it, while the grouping entity is used to show a group of two people; however the communications of those people feed the communication mixture entity. Again, the output of the communication mixture entity includes the total communications of those three people. The second diagram below is the same as the first one, except *group* is being replaced by the plus sign instead. It does not matter; we can always change the text in an entity.

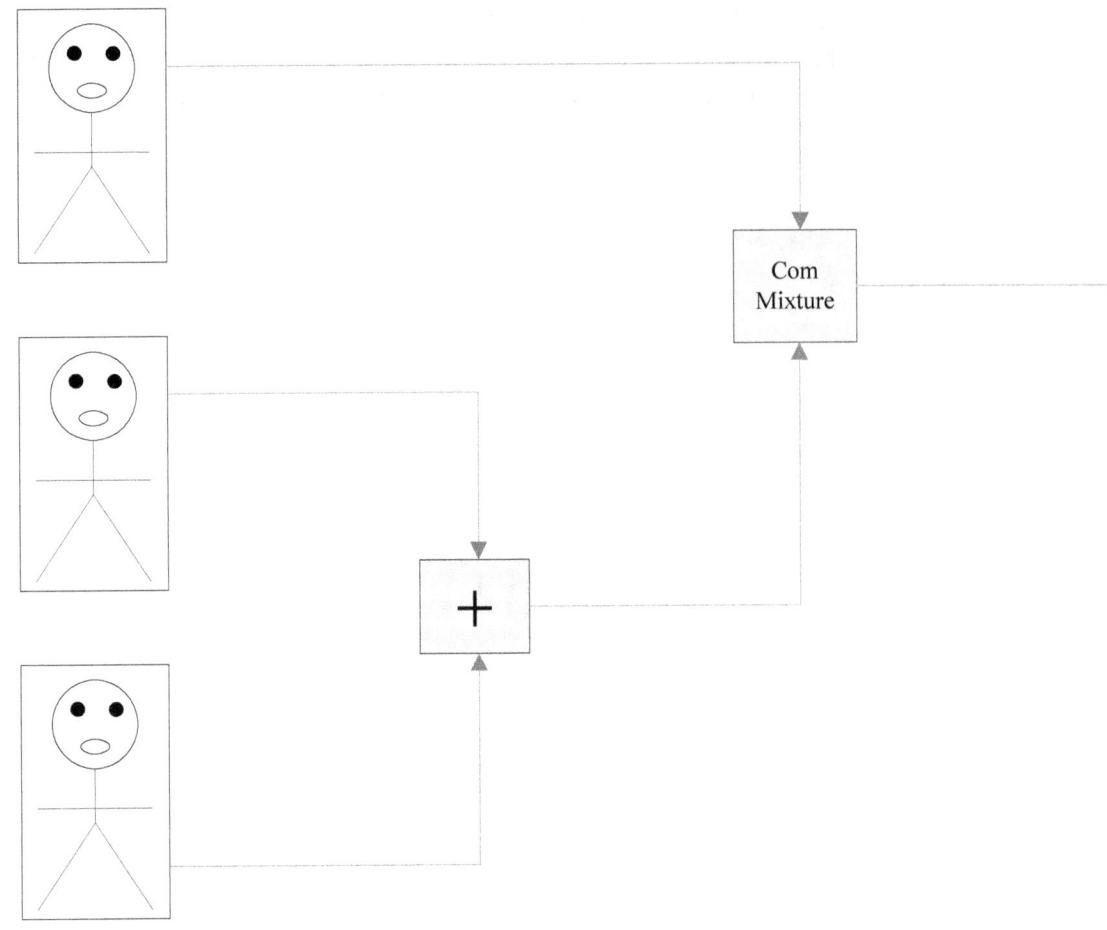

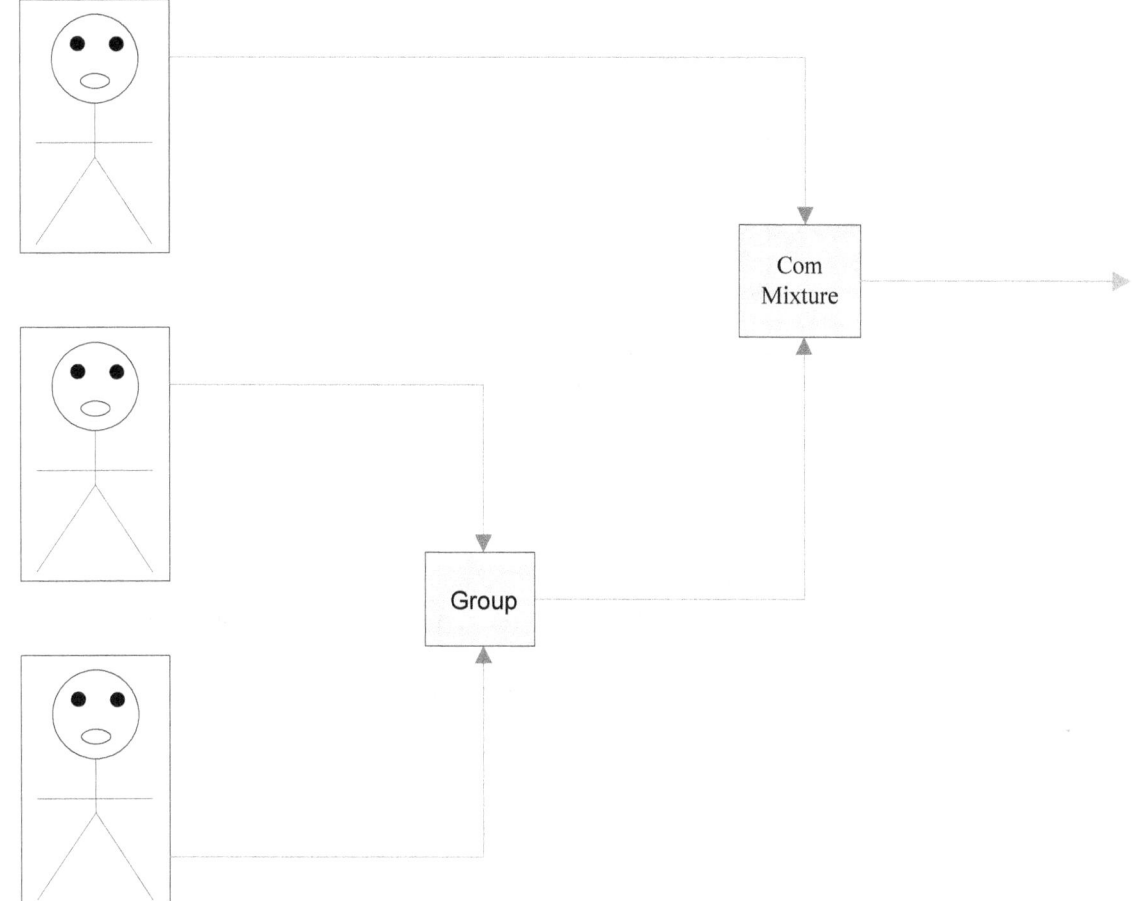

Example Number 11

We can use timeline in conjunction with dateline to show specific statement or question at a given date or time. Below is an example of using the time chart with the dateline to record statements and questions. From the diagram below, Date 1 is the recorded date for statement 1 and 2, while Date 2 is the recorded date for question 1 and 2.

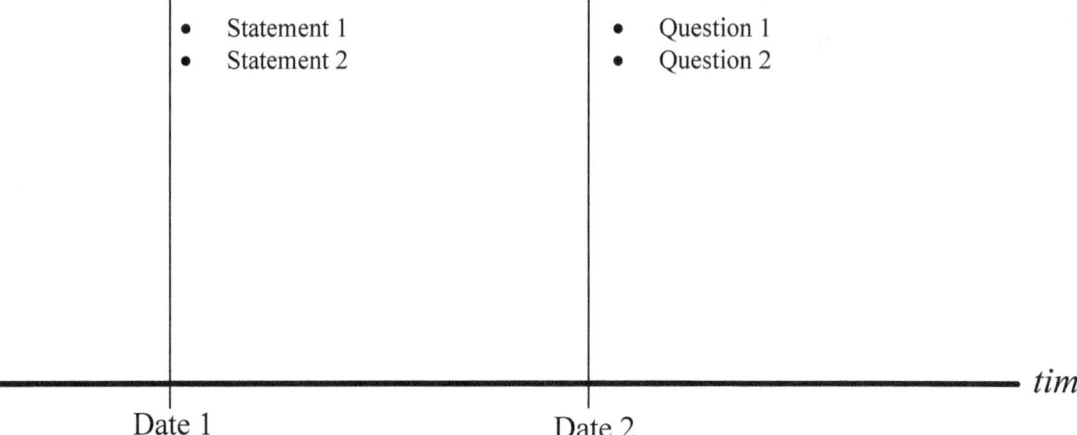

- Statement 1
- Statement 2

- Question 1
- Question 2

Date 1   Date 2

tim

Example Number 12

The diagram below shows the starting communication of two people that extends to four people. As usual, the output of the communication mixture entity includes the total communications of the people that feed that communication mixture. The last output of the communication mixture entity includes the communications of all people in the project or that communication. The diagram below shows a total communication of four people. To reduce space, we can group some of those people together. The second diagram below simply shows the grouping of three of those people. Keep in mind that the second diagram is the same as the first one, except in the second diagram we group some of those people together. The output of the communication mixture is still the same. The third diagram below is the same, except we use the linear form of grouping.

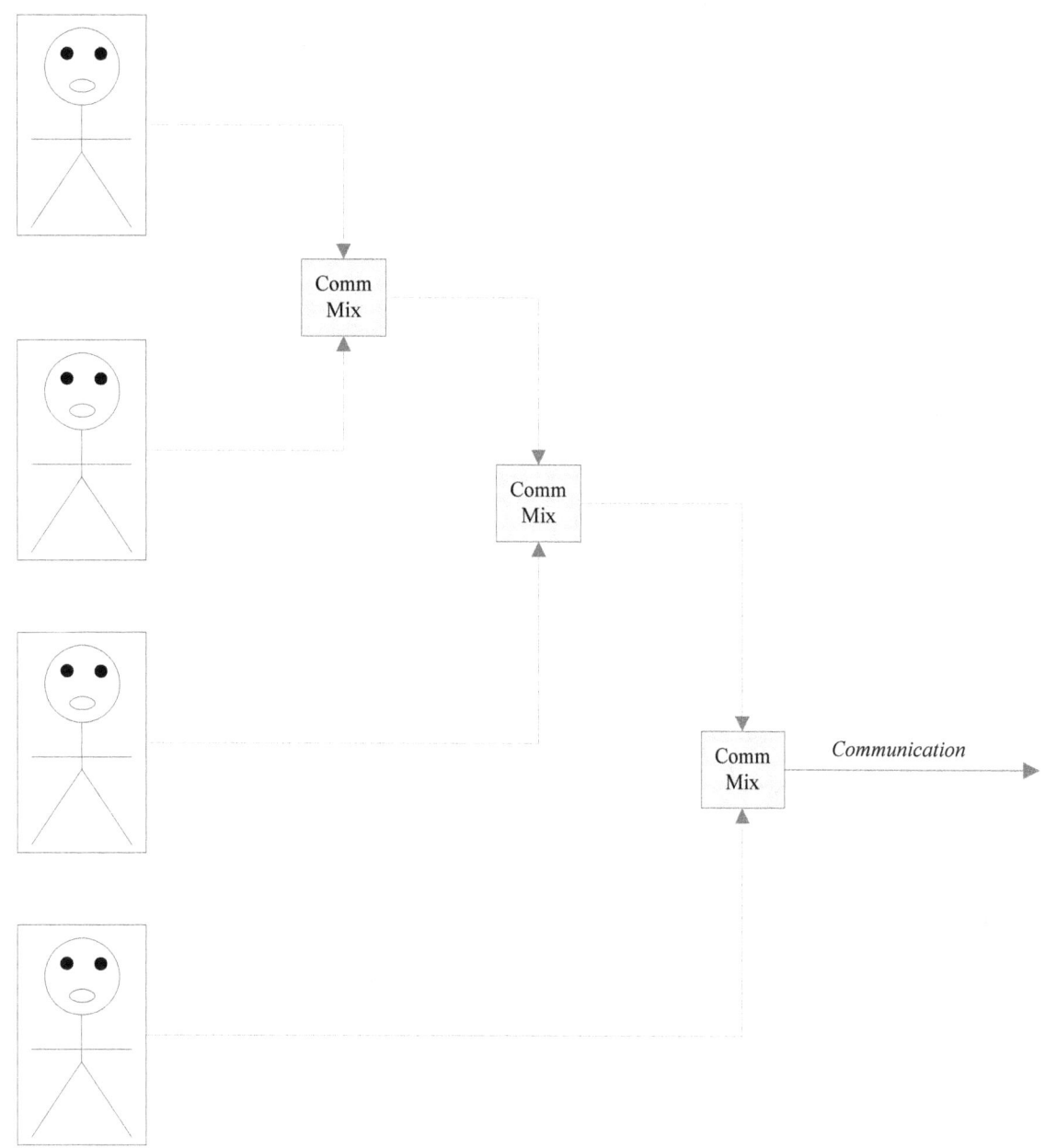

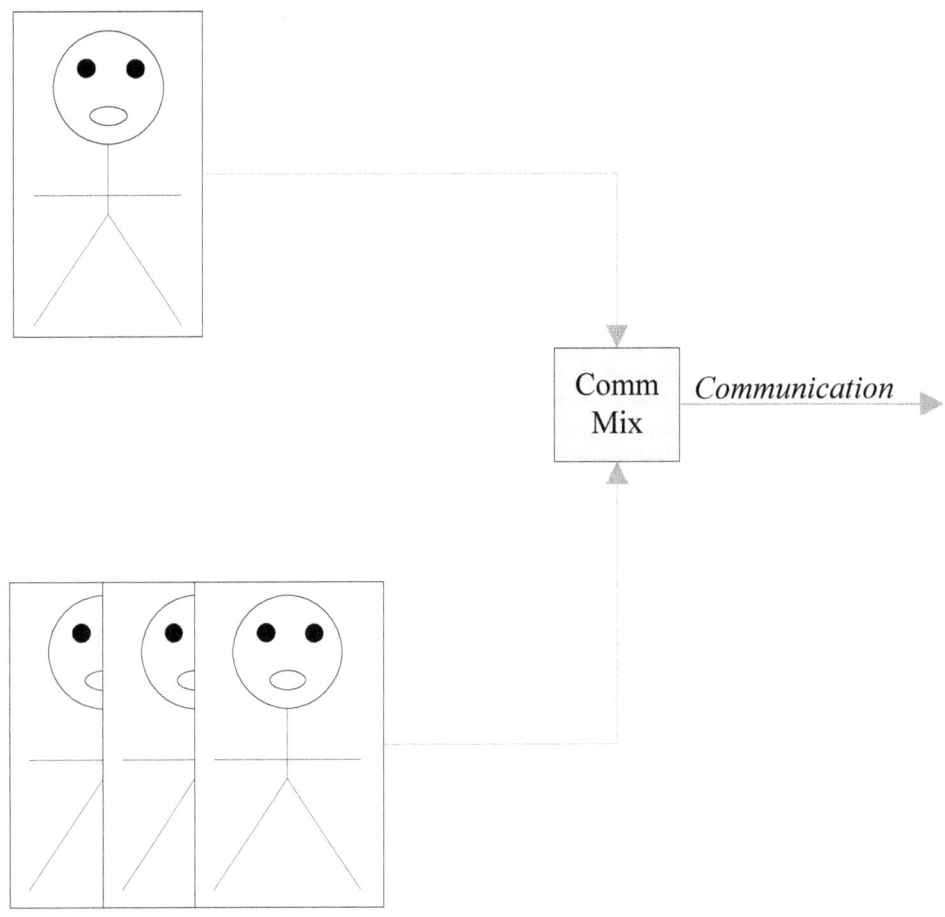

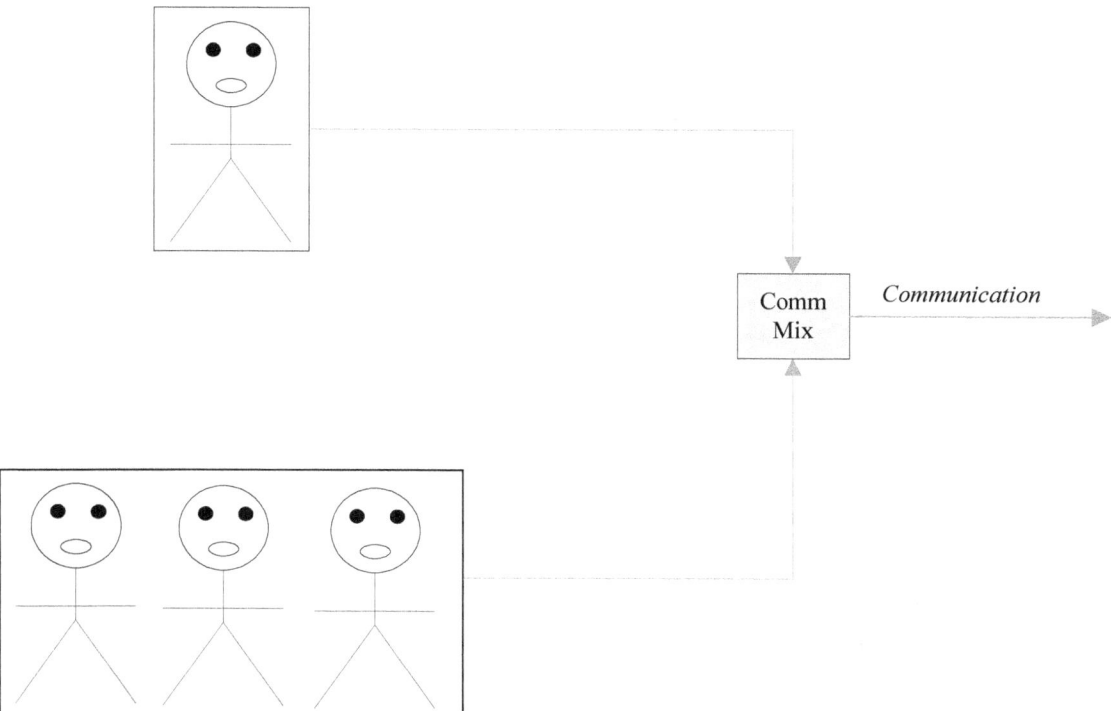

Example Number 13

Assume that our application is divided into two parts, we can use part of the application entity to show that. The diagram below shows that our project is made up three employees, where the application is separated into two parts.

Application

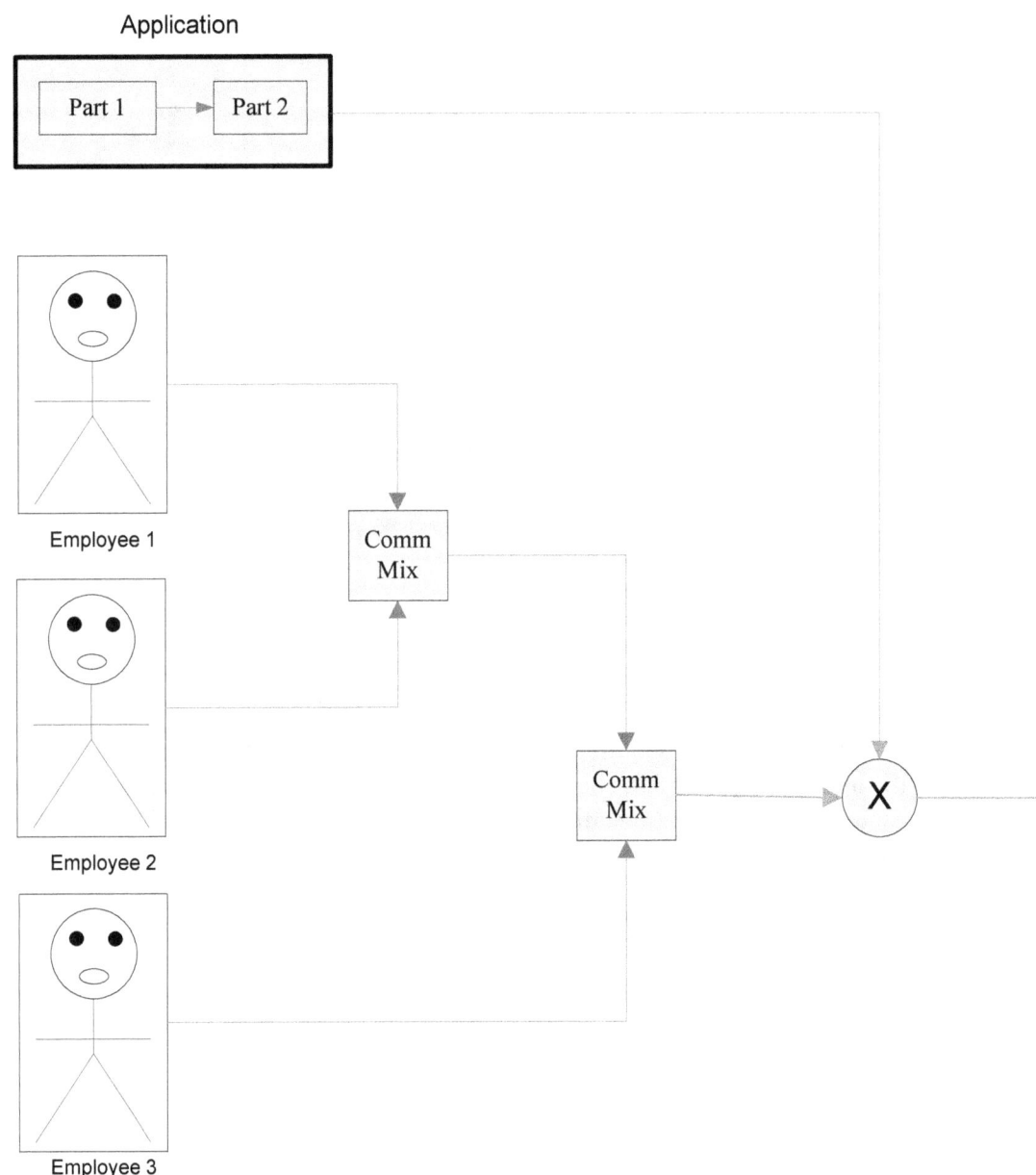

The diagram above can also be represented in this form

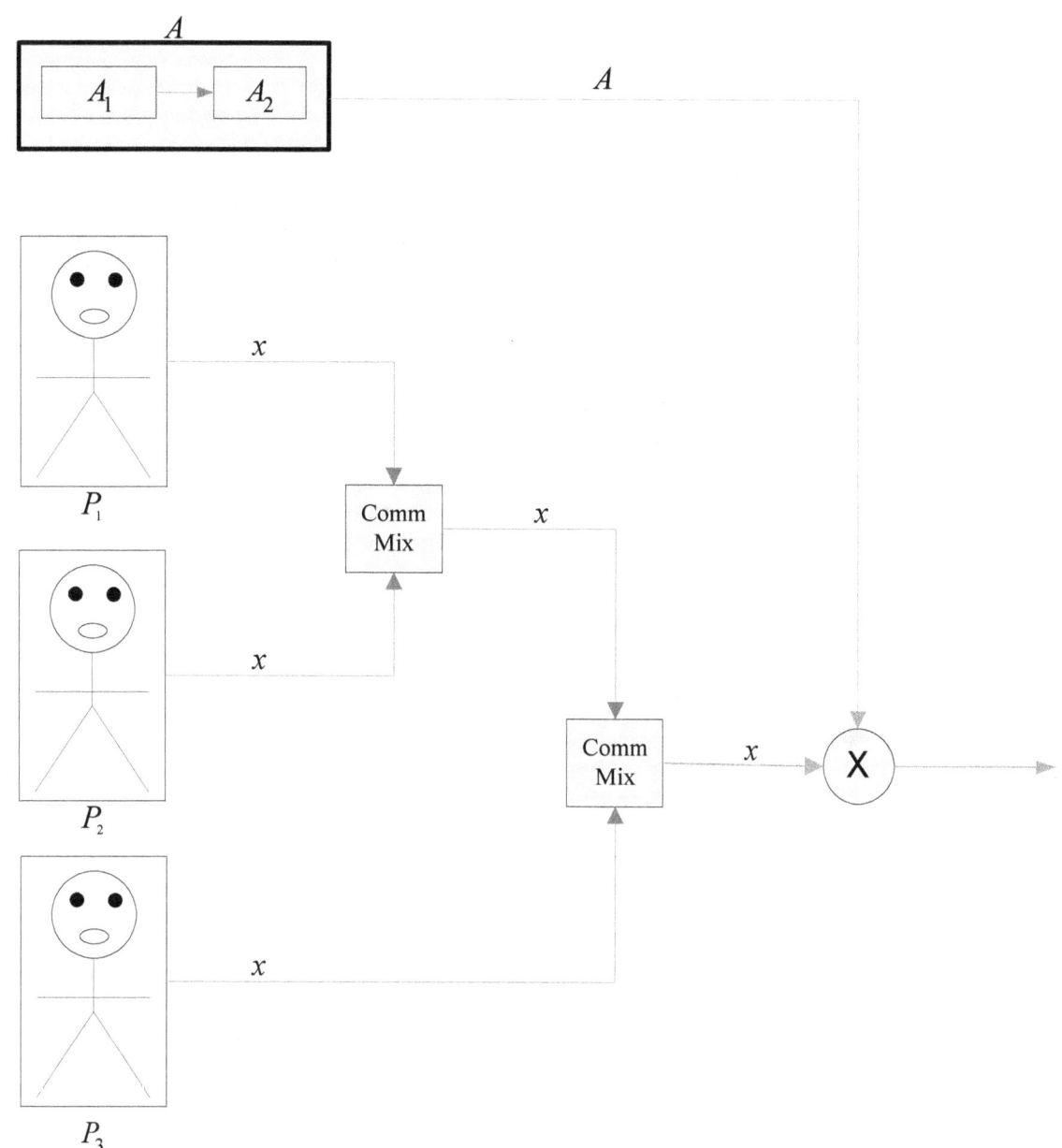

Example Number 14
This example is similar to the one above; except that employee number 3 is being replaced by a communication holder and part 1 of the application also include other parts. In this case, it looks like part 1 of the application is viewed as a sub application. The way to look at it, while employee three is being worked in a project that has different parts; but employee three can also be worked in another part of the project. Since employee three cannot be duplicated physically, in this case when the whole project is being viewed in the same sheet or on the same screen, it makes sense for employee three to be replaced by his/her respective communication holder. For instance if we model our project on a piece of paper, where employee three has two functions in different section of the project, when both sections are being viewed in a single sheet or on the same screen, in one section employee three is replaced by his/her respective communication holder as shown below.

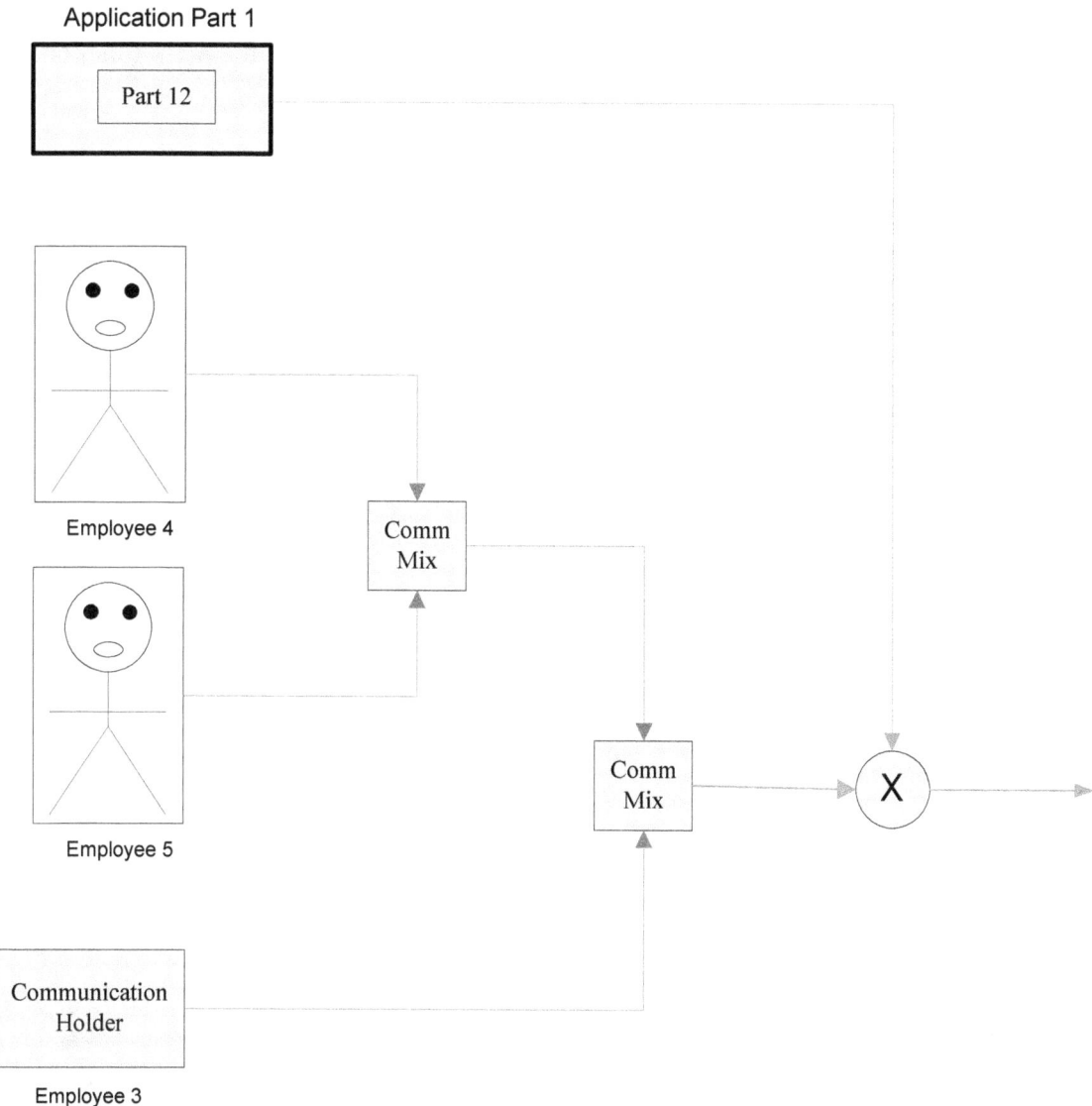

Application Part 1

Part 12

Employee 4

Employee 5

Comm Mix

Comm Mix

X

Communication Holder

Employee 3

Example Number 15

This example is similar to the one above. In this example, the
communication function includes a sub function, where the sub function
can be viewed as function 2. We can use sub function to group part of the

communication function that can be outside of the main function. We can also use them to show functions that are also parts of the main function.

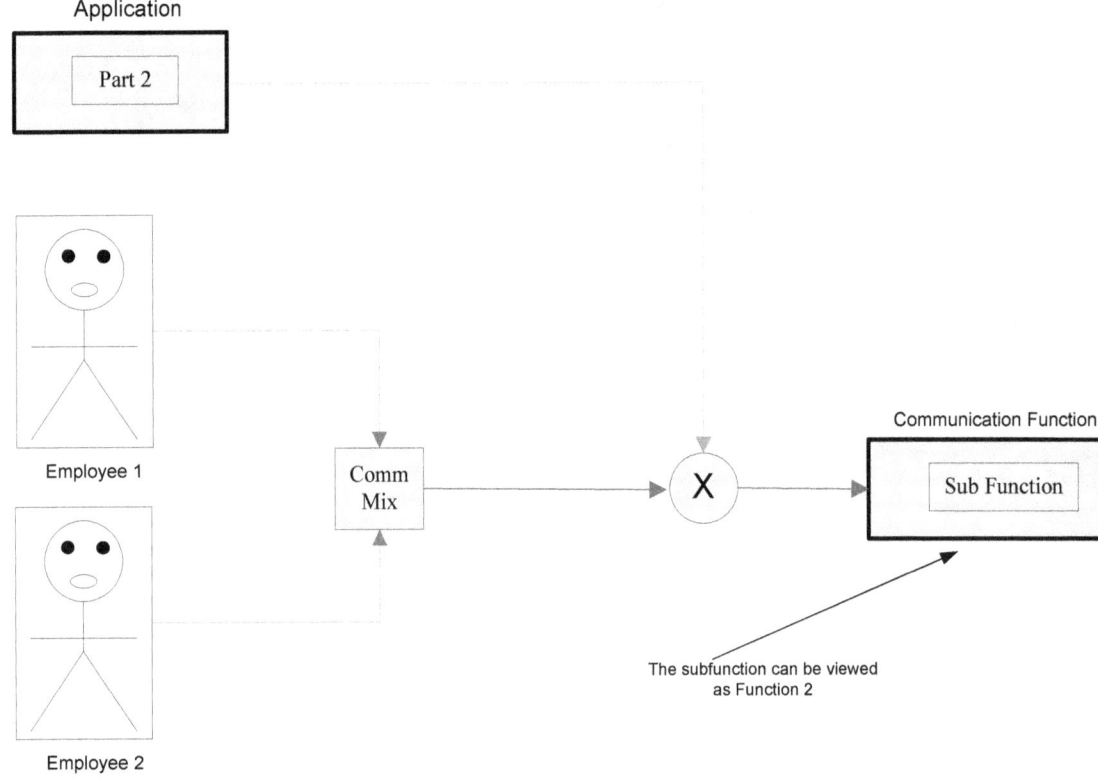

From the diagram above, the sub function is considered to be function 2. Now, we can expand the sub function to show more information about this section of the project. By doing so, we can also see the part of the application is also expanded with the sub function. In this example, part 2 of the application is also linked to function 2, where function 2 is considered the main communication function for that part of application. Our diagram below assumes that our project is made of several sections. In this case, each section can lead or managed by different people. For this reason, it makes sense to have sub functions, part of functions, sub results, parts of result, sub applications, and parts of application.

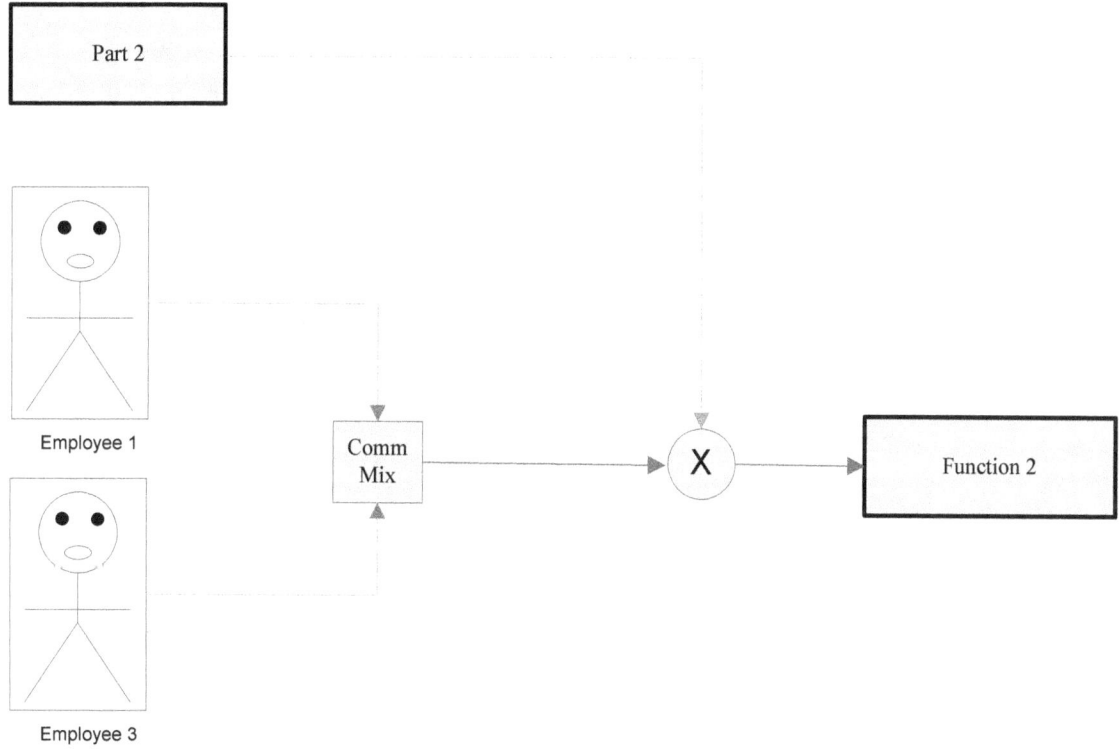

The diagram below is also another way of looking at the diagram above. If we assume that employee 1 can be working on a different part of the project, but managed by another person. In this case, when viewing both diagrams together, it makes sense for employee 1 to be replaced by his/her respective communication holder. Assume that employee one is working and managed by one person, but helping out another project that is managed by another person. In this case, when both projects are linked together and being viewed in the same screen or paper, in one of them, mostly the second one, employee 1 will definitely be replaced by his/her communication holder. The diagram below simply shows that. While we say help out in another project, we mean help out in another part of the project. It is always good to view the overall project as a single project that has different parts, but managed by different people.

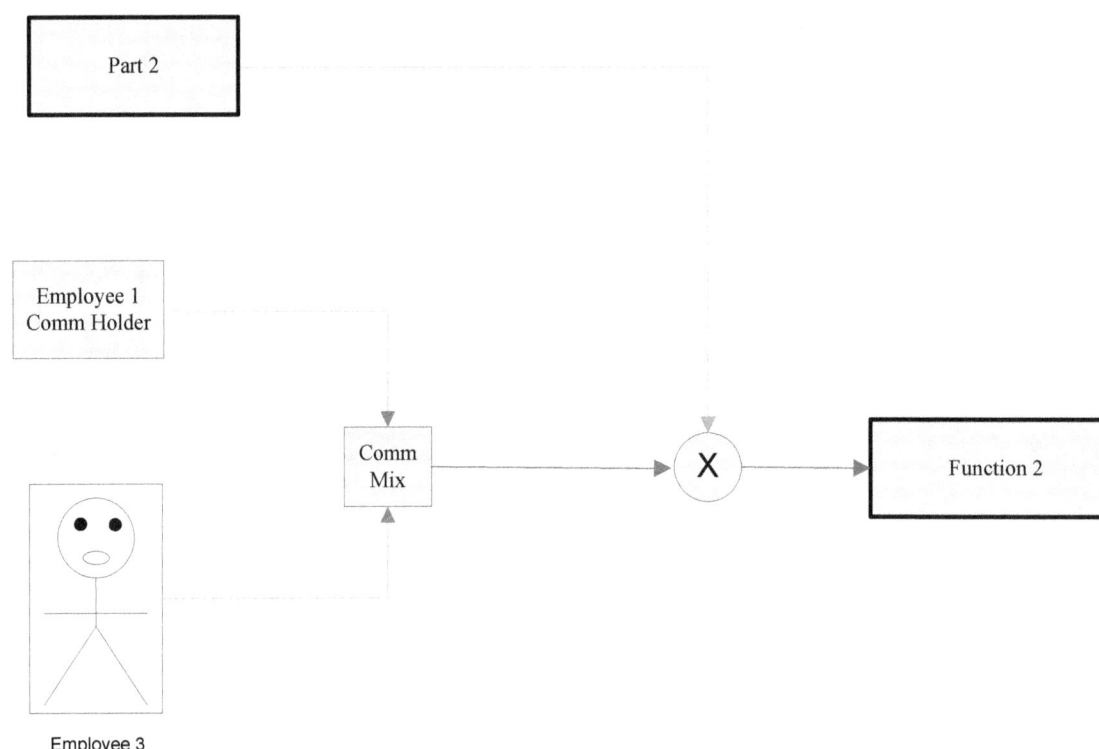

Example Number 16

In a project, it may be possible for us to use communication of people that are not physically in the project. The external communication holder enables us to do so. It is very important for us to take communication into consideration in our project. The external communication holder can hold communications from external sources. For instance people, books, magazine articles, newsletters, interviews etc. The diagram below shows the usage of the external communication holder. In this case, it shows the communication of a person that is not physically in the project. While that person is not in the project, however its communication contributes to the project.

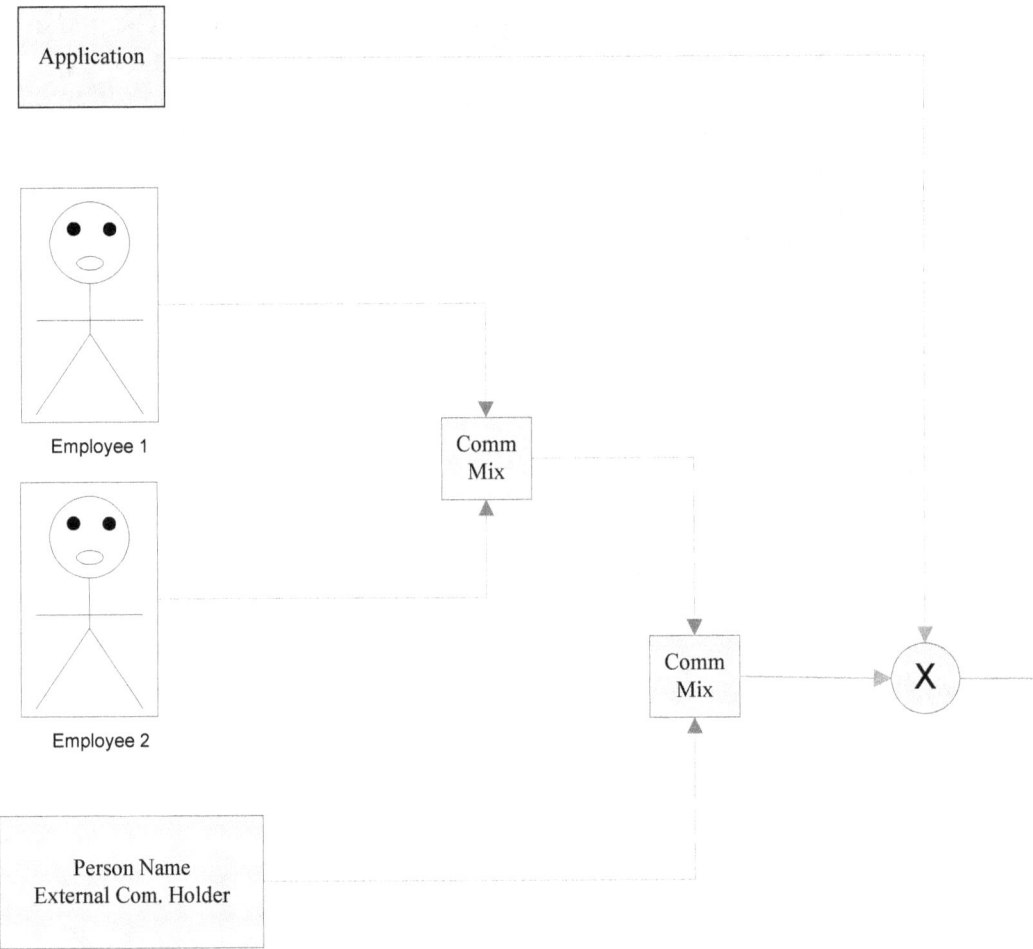

The diagram below is similar to the one above, except the external
communication holder holds communication from a magazine article.
Since our project can contain communication from different sources, in
this case we use that magazine article in our project. That magazine
article can contain information that enables us to execute the overall
function of the project, which is the communication function. That
magazine article can also affect the result of the project. It is very
important to take external communications into consideration in term of
analysis.

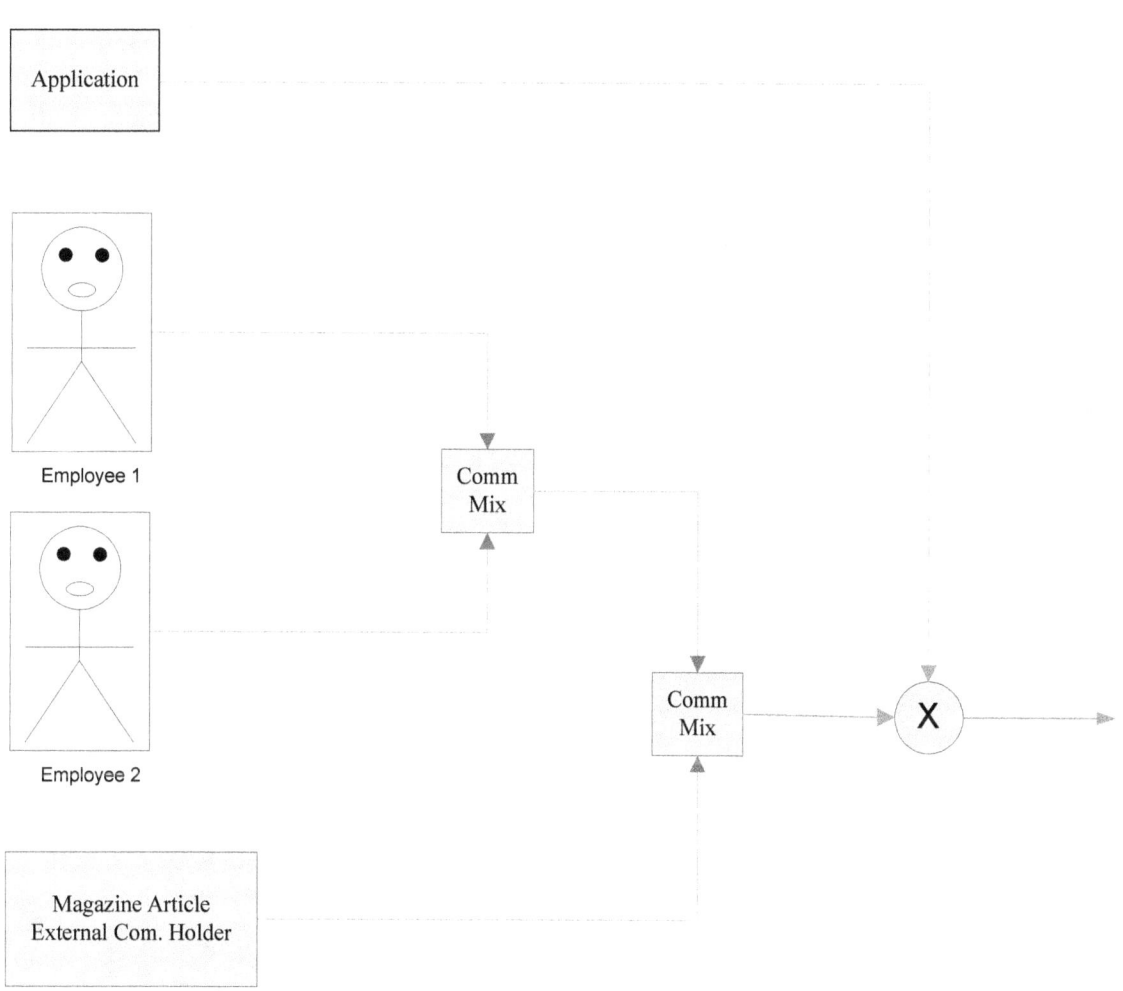

Application

Employee 1

Employee 2

Comm
Mix

Comm
Mix

X

Magazine Article
External Com. Holder

Since external communication holders are considered to be entities, they can also be grouped by using the grouping entity. From the diagram below, we use the grouping entity to group two external communication holders. Since the project we are working on depends on what we need to do, there is not limit on how many external communication holders that can be used. Assume that we are working in a project where information from a book and one from a magazine article, we can group both of them to show that. We can also group them together as long as they can be combined to enable us to do what we do. From the diagram below, we group two external communication holders. In this case, we assume that both of them are related to enable us to do what we do. The second diagram below is the same as the first one, except we use the communication mixture for the two external communication holders rather than using the grouping entity. Since external communication holders are considered to be communication themselves, they can be mixed together using the communication mixture entity.

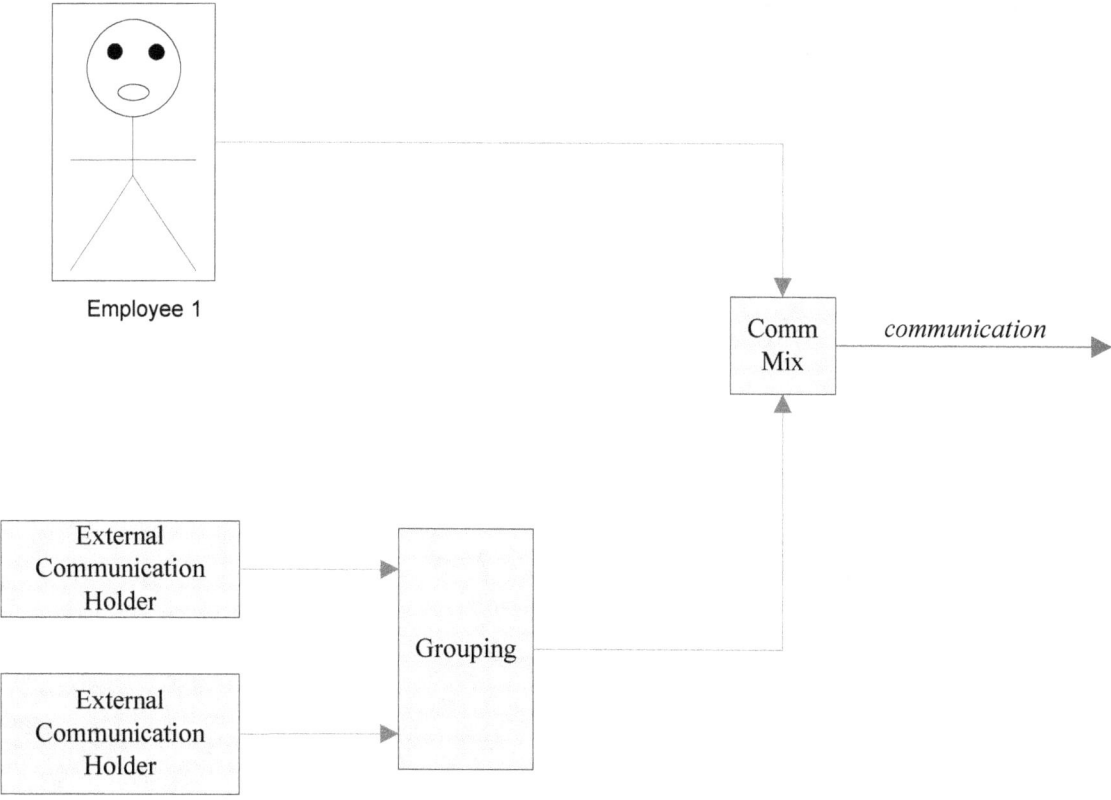

Employee 1

External Communication Holder

External Communication Holder

Grouping

Comm Mix

communication

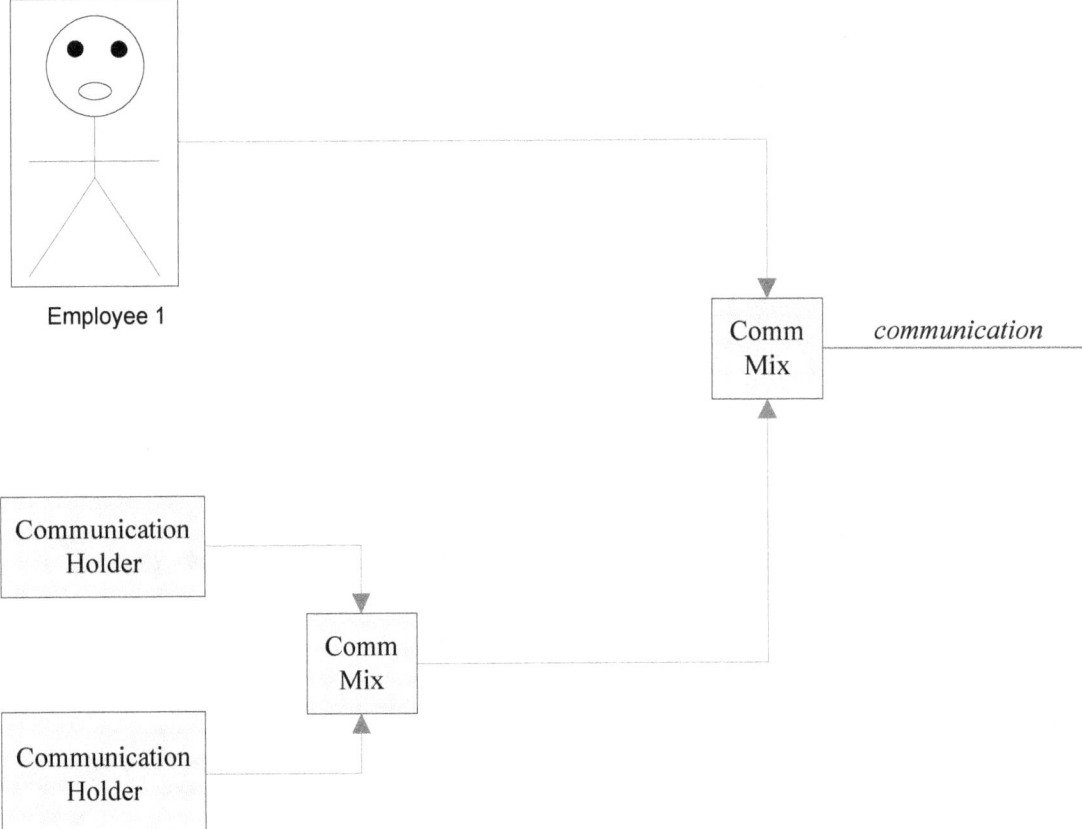

Employee 1

Communication Holder

Comm Mix

Communication Holder

Comm Mix

communication

Since communication holders are considered to be entities themselves, they can be grouped in the same form as we group entities. The diagrams below show another way of grouping external communication holders and communication holders. We can use this form of grouping in order to preserve space.

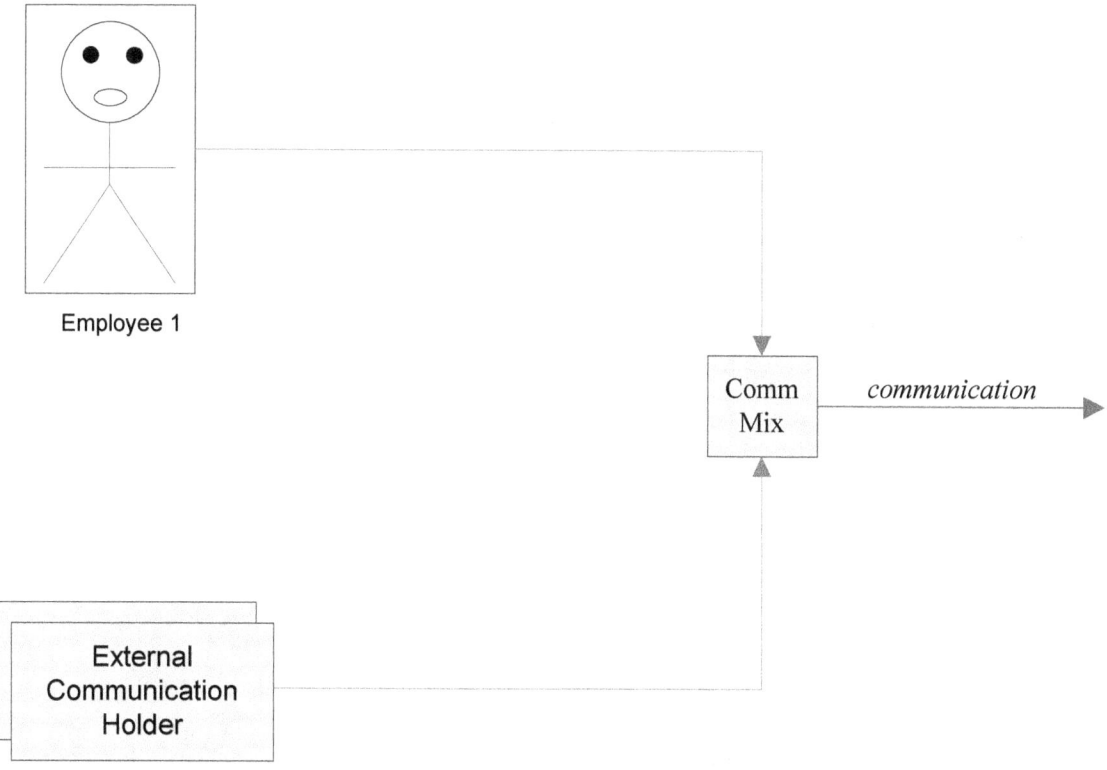

Employee 1

Comm
Mix

communication

External
Communication
Holder

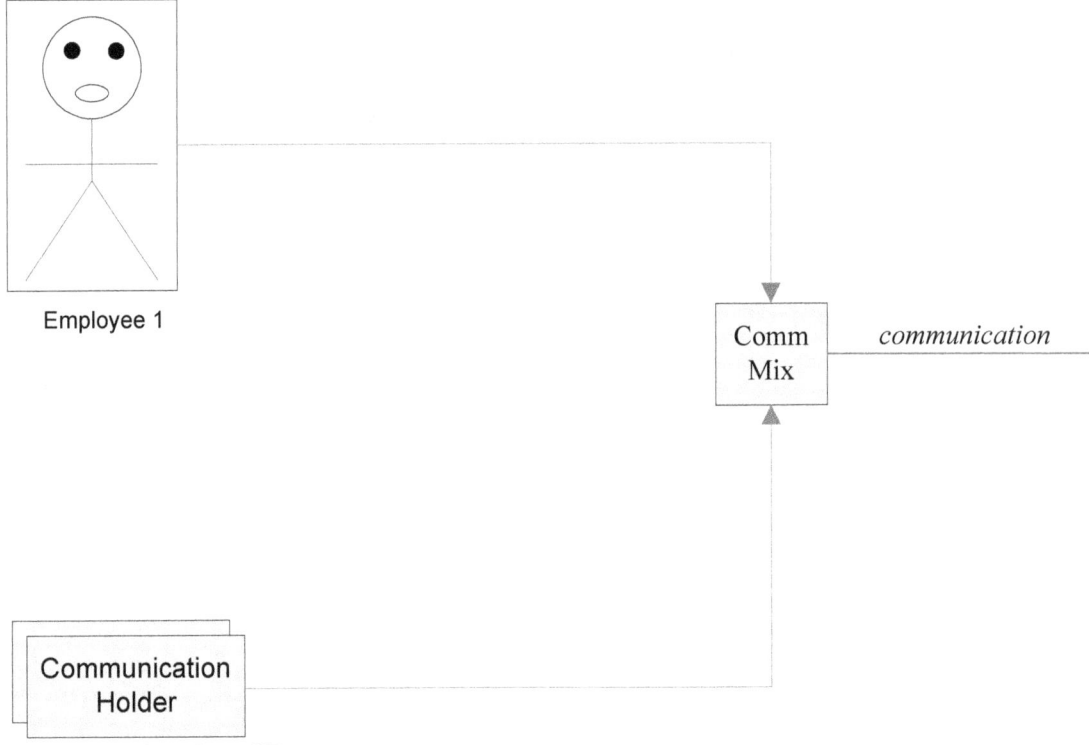

Employee 1

Comm Mix

communication

Communication Holder

Example Number 17

Within a conversation or a communication, we can recall an important part of that communication. Within a communication or a conversation, we can recall and important point of that communication. We use the callout to show an important point of a communication or a conversation. Assume that two employees are communicating together about a project, if one of the employees record an important point of that conversation, then a callout can be used to show that. Whenever we use the term important point, we use a part of the communication that is important to the project or the employees for instance. In the diagram below, we use callouts to record important parts of the communication by the employees.

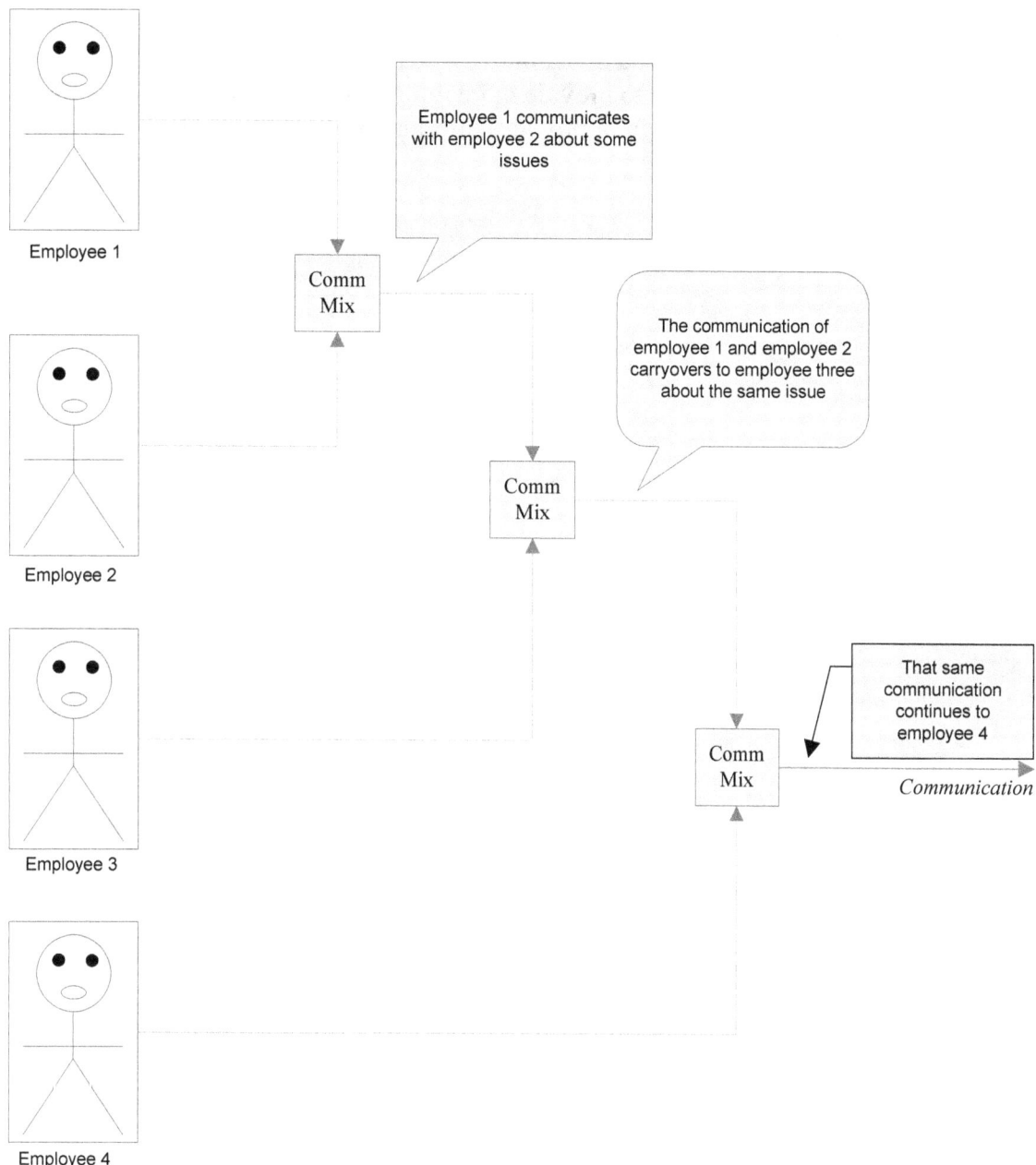

Employee 1

Employee 2

Employee 3

Employee 4

Comm Mix

Employee 1 communicates with employee 2 about some issues

Comm Mix

The communication of employee 1 and employee 2 carryovers to employee three about the same issue

Comm Mix

That same communication continues to employee 4

Communication

If we don't want to use callouts to show important points of a conversation or communication, we can also use node with numbers to show that. The diagram below is the same as the one above, except nodes with numbers are being used instead of callouts. When we use nodes with numbers, we can also use a table to provide more information about those nodes. The table below the diagram provides information about the nodes.

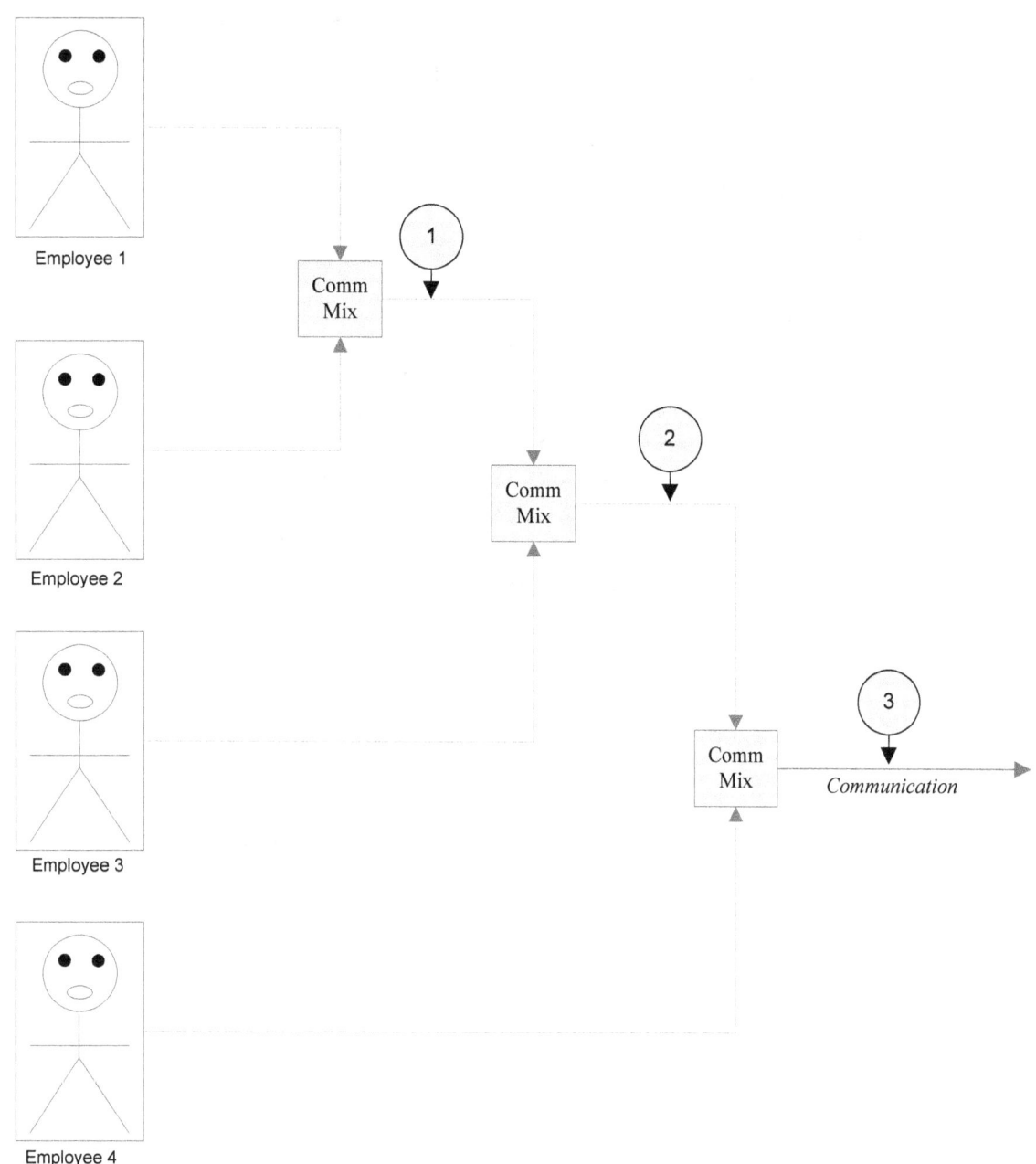

Employee 1

Employee 2

Employee 3

Employee 4

Comm Mix

1

Comm Mix

2

Comm Mix

3

Communication

Node Number	1	2	3
Node Information	Employee 1 communicates with employee 2 about an issue	That same communication carryovers to employee 3 about the same issue	The communication continues to employee 4

Example Number 18
While we use words for oral and written communications, however we don't think about them directly. We think about actual entities they represent. For instance, if we use the word *table* we think about an actual table, which is a physical table. If we use the word *tree*, we think about a tree which is a physical entity. The point to label or the point to arrow label enables us to map a word with the actual entity it represents. From the diagrams below, we show the usage of the point to label, where we show each actual entity each word represents.

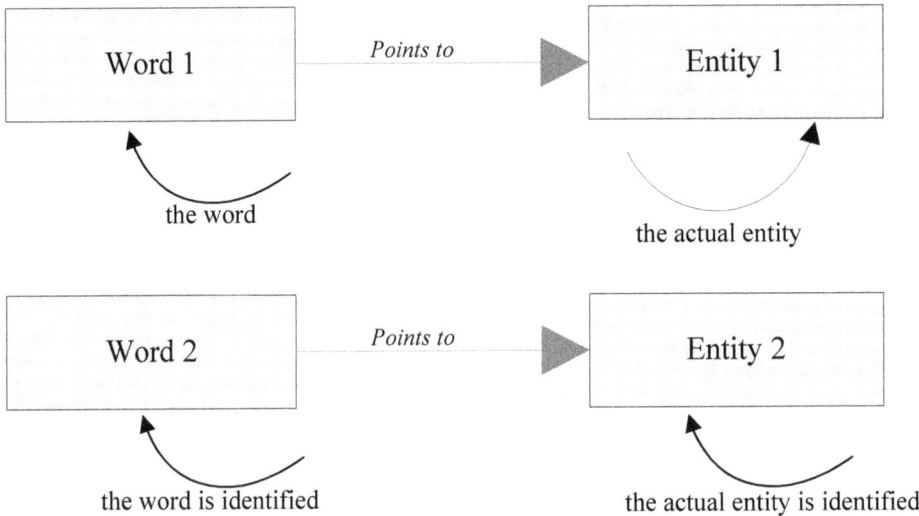

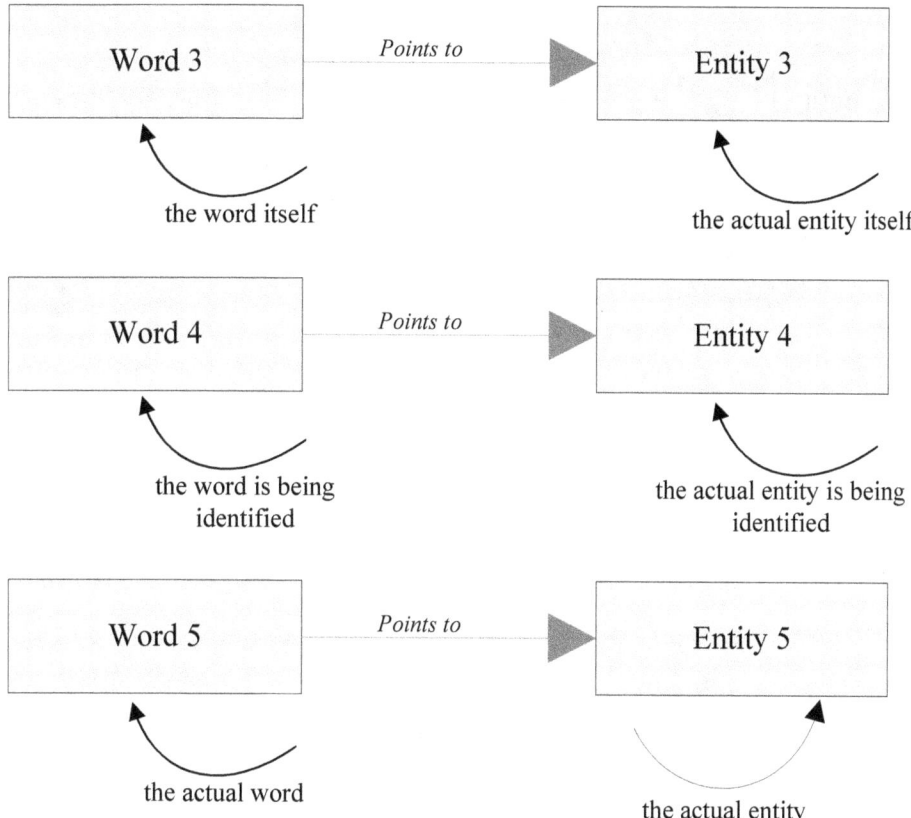

| Word 3 | *Points to* → | Entity 3 |

the word itself — the actual entity itself

| Word 4 | *Points to* → | Entity 4 |

the word is being identified — the actual entity is being identified

| Word 5 | *Points to* → | Entity 5 |

the actual word — the actual entity

Example Number 19

Within a project, it may be important for us to show actual entities that we use for the project. Assume that in our project it is required for us to use physical entities, it may be possible for us to show the usage of those entities related to the project. In this case, we can group those entities to show their quantities. The diagram below shows the usage of entities in our project. We can only do that if it is desired. In the diagram below, we use the grouping entity to group the entities.

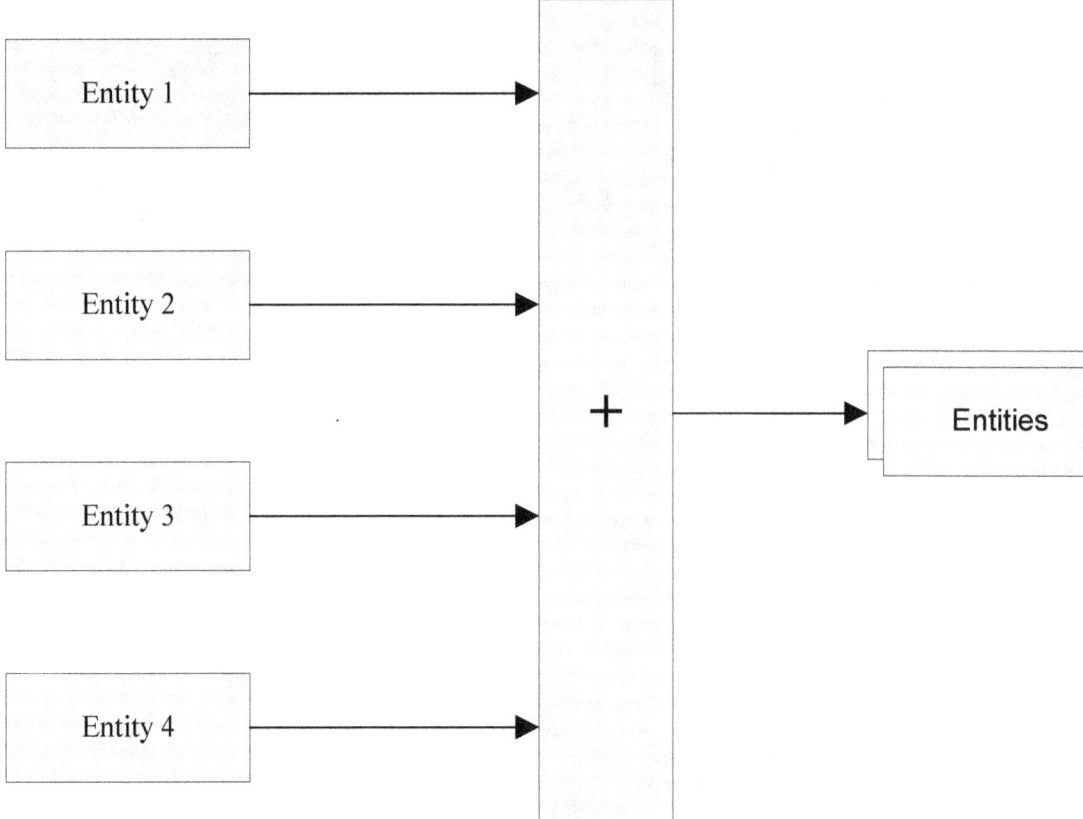

To preserve space, we can also use the grouping entities in the form of one on top each other to show the grouping of the entities. The diagram below shows a different way of grouping the entities to the left. This diagram is the same as the one above, except we group the last three entities in the left in order to reduce space.

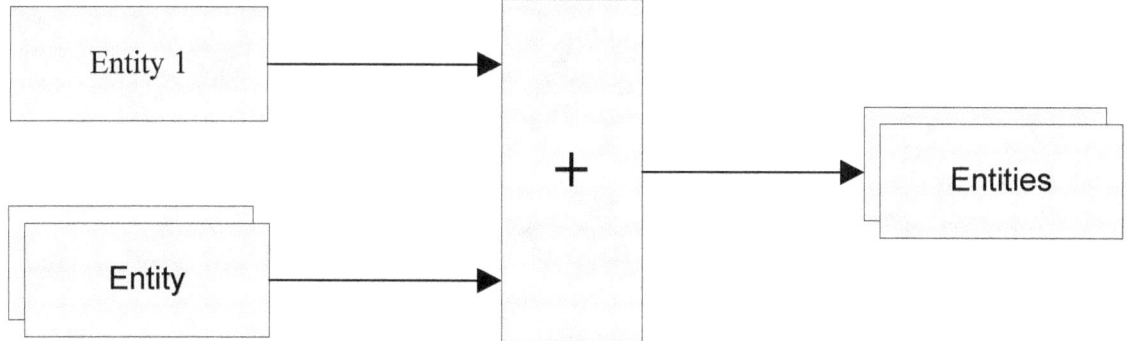

Example Number 20
Since problems are considered to be entities themselves, they can also be grouped. Within our project, it maybe possible and require for us to show all the problems we have in the project. By grouping all the problems we have together, we show the total problems we have in the project. The diagram below shows the grouping of the problem we have in the project. We use the grouping entity to group the problems.

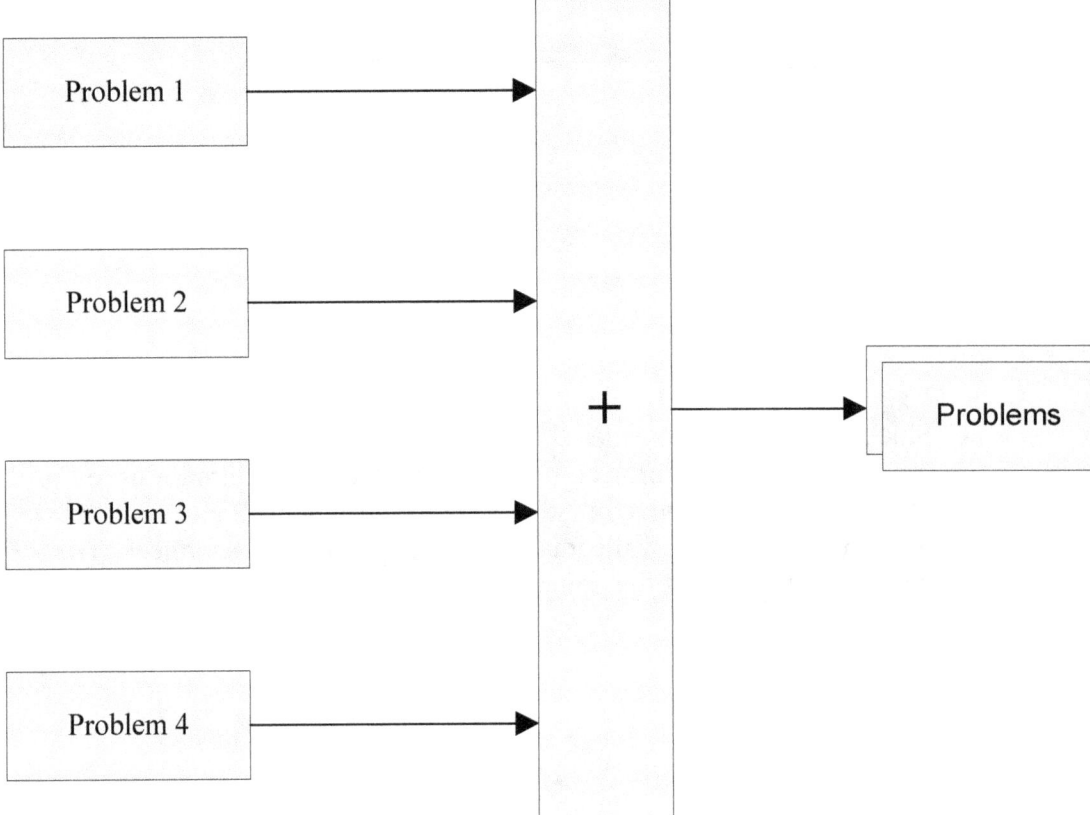

As we did for the entity grouping diagram, we can also do the same for problems. To preserve space, we have grouped the last four problems in the left above in a form of one on each other. The result gives us the diagram below. Disregard the way we group them, the output is always the total problem for the project.

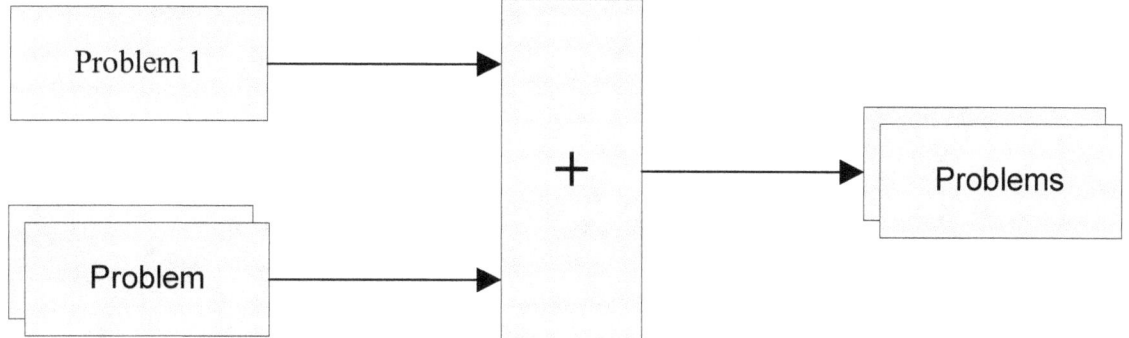

Example Number 21

Since error in communication gives rise to problem, an error that occurs in a project can develop problems, it may be important for us to accumulate all errors in our project so we can keep track of them. The diagram below shows a way for us to group our errors in our project. We use the grouping entity to group the errors.

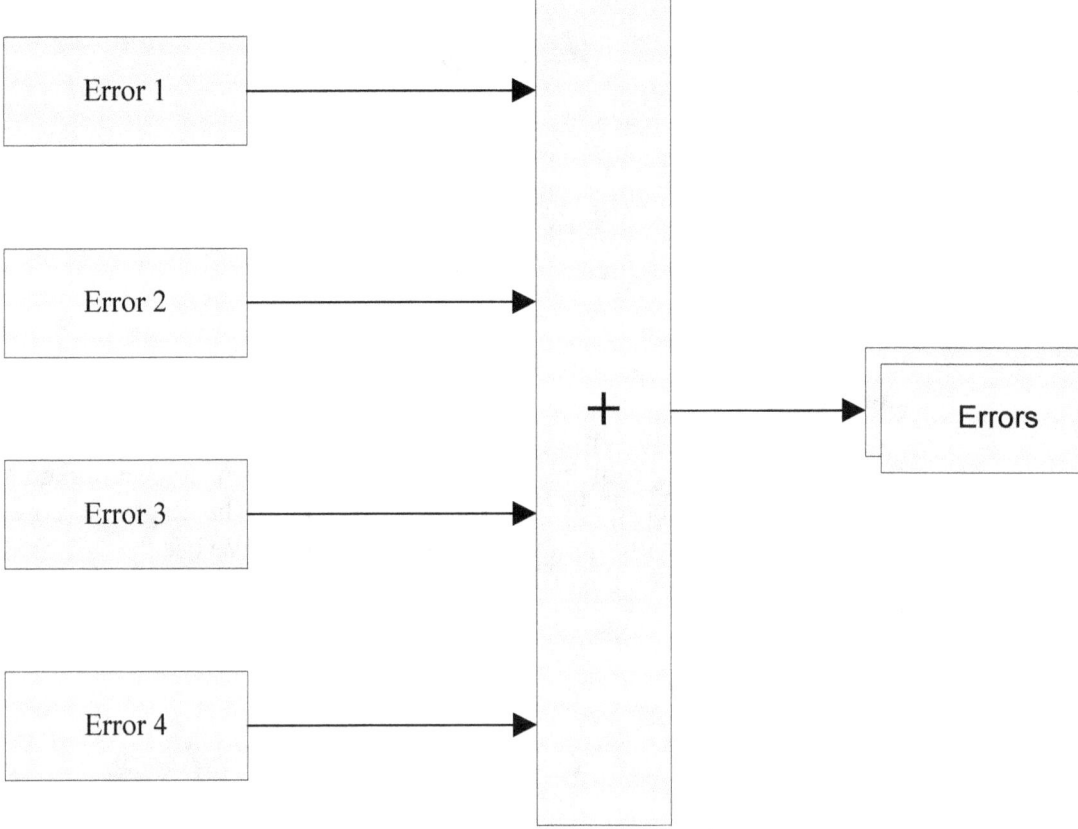

To reduce space, we can also group errors in a form where we can show one on top of each other. The diagram below shows that form of grouping error. This diagram is simply the same as the one above, except the last three errors in the bottom are being grouped to form a single one. The result is still the total error for the project.

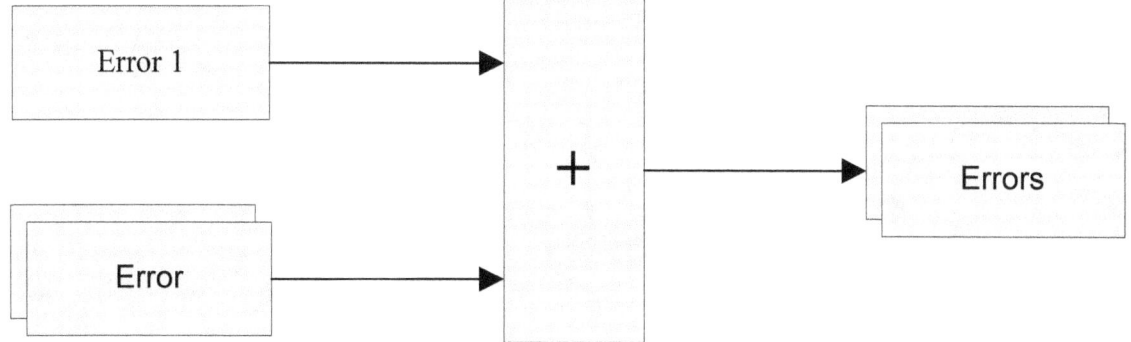

Example Number 22
It may be important for us in a project to track all the feedbacks that we receive for the project. In this case, we can group all the feedbacks so we can keep track of them. By using the grouping entity in the form showing above, we can group all the feedbacks we receive in our project. The diagram below shows the total feedback of the project.

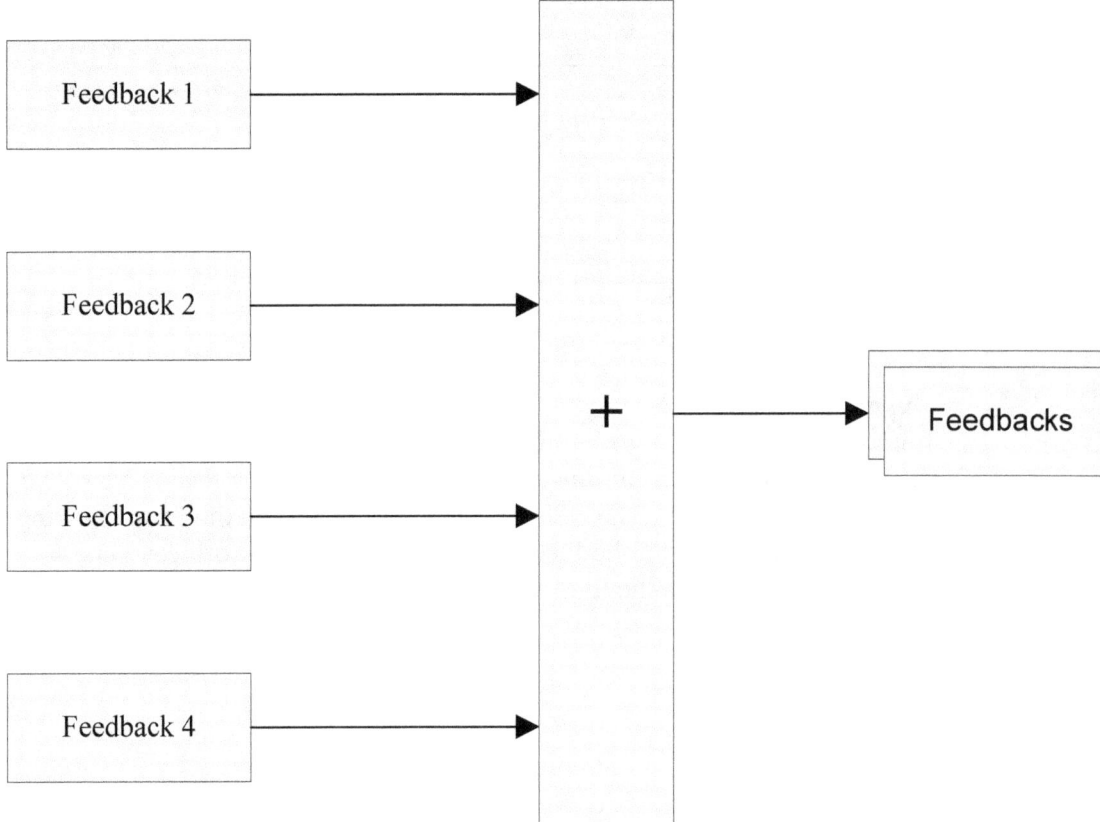

While we use the diagram below to sum all the feedbacks we have received in the project, to reduce space, we can also group them in a form of one over each other. The diagram below is the same as the one above, except we group the last three feedback one on top of each other. The output still provides the total feedback.

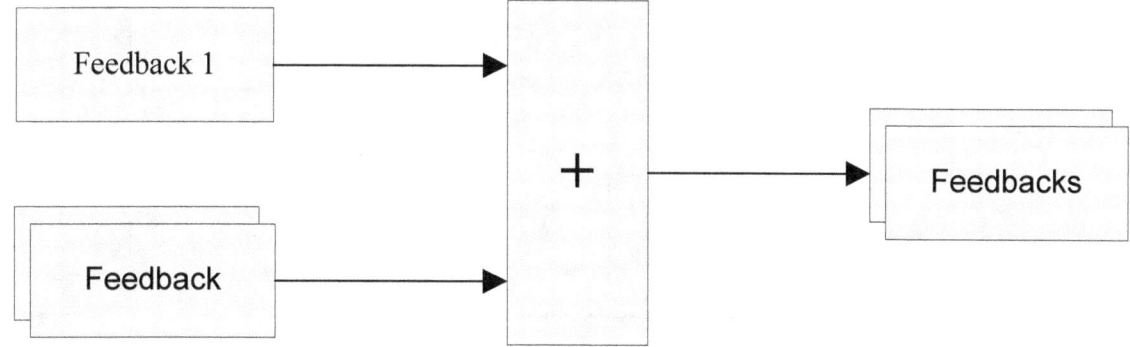

Example Number 23

We can use timeline and dateline to show our project timeline and our project schedule. The diagram below shows the usage of timeline and dateline to show a project schedule. While we use number with the date to show specific date, it does not matter. The date can be any date that is related to the project.

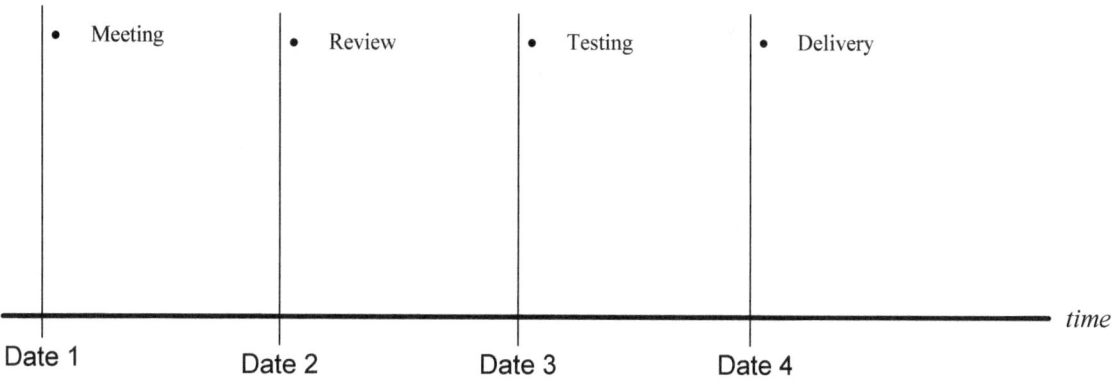

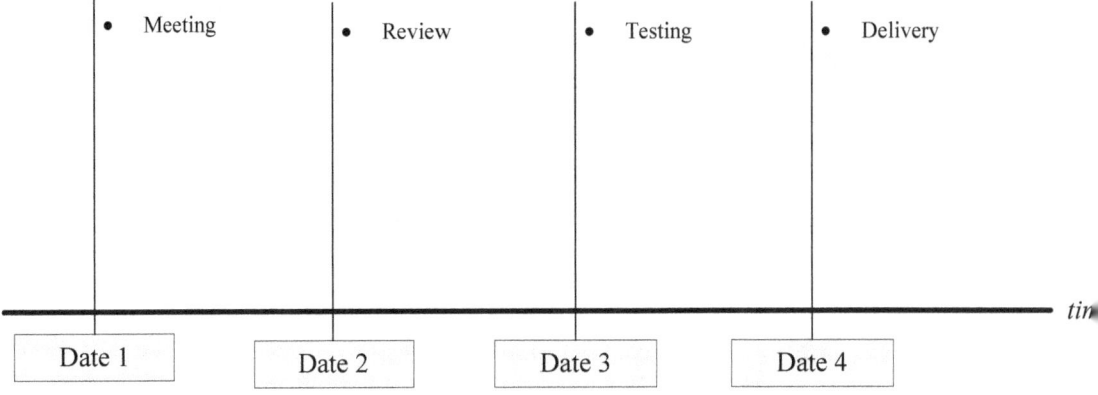

Example Number 24

Assume that we are working in a project, where we have 50 people in our project. Now while modeling our project, it may not be possible for us to show all of them. For instance, assume that we are modeling our project in a piece of paper or a drawing board, for illustration purpose, we may not want to show all of them. In this case, we can use continuity in this form to show the people in our project. For the first diagram, the continuity means there are some other people after *Person 3*, while in the second diagram, the continuity means there are some other people between *Person 2* and *Person 50*.

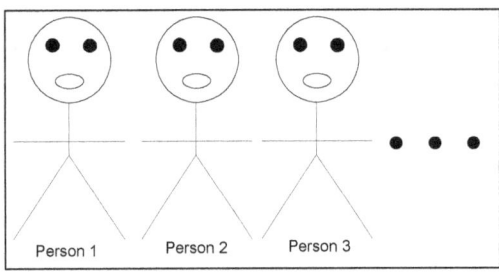 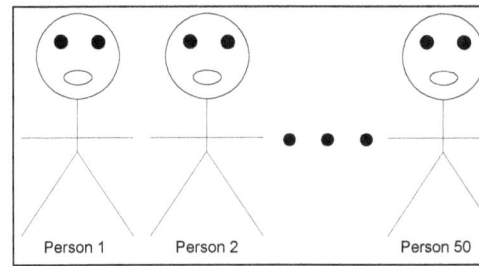

We can also use continuity to show the continuity of parts of our communication function and also the continuity of part of our application. The diagram below shows what we are talking about. Assume that we are working in a project, where our communication function is made of 10

different functions. In this case, we can show them in the following form. Assume that we have limited space to show all the functions, here we use continuity to show there are some functions between the last one that are not listed.

Communication Function

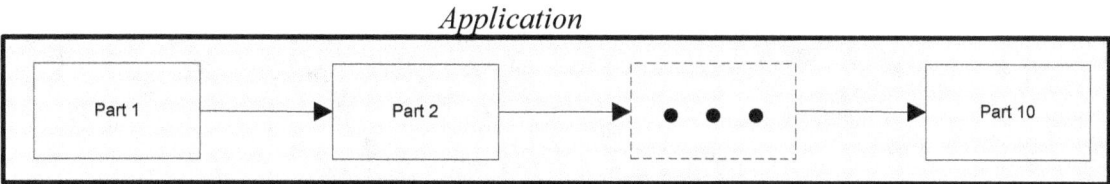

As we did for the communication function above, we can also do similarly for the parts of application and any other entity that can be used with continuity. Assume that we are working in a project, where our application is made of 10 parts; in this case we can use continuity if we don't want to show all of them as shown by the diagram below.

Application

Example Number 25
Since references contain information, it maybe possible for references to be given to us at a time we can use it and when it is necessary. The reference entity can be used in the form below to show a reference given from one person to another person.

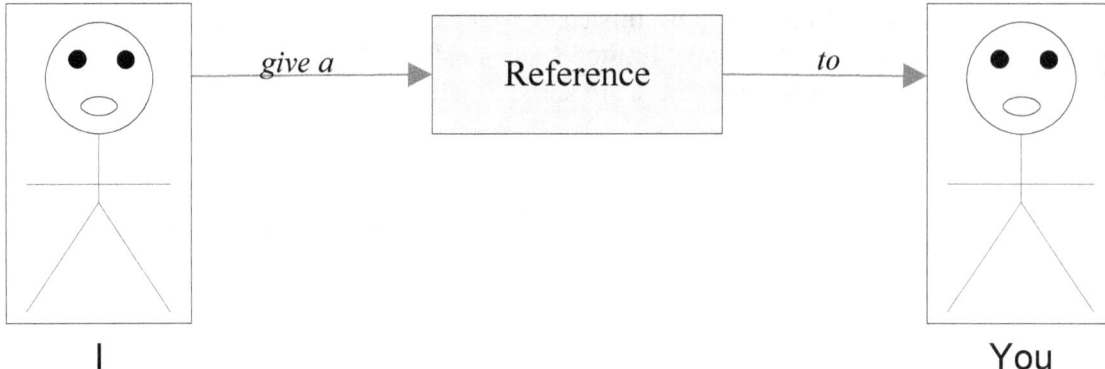

I   You

Since not all entities are considered to be references and the principles attached to a reference must be understood in order for a given entity to be considered to be a reference, it may be possible for one to present an entity to others that is not a reference. For that reason, feedback can be used as shown below with the reference entity to determine if that entity is an actual reference.

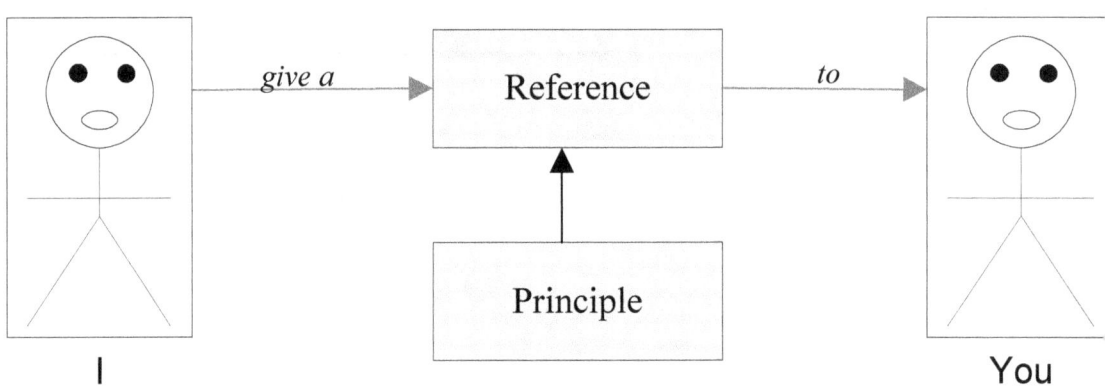

I   You

Since a reference is given in the form of communication, during our communication it is possible for a reference to be given and it is also possible for a reference to be captured. The diagram below shows that a reference is given during a communication.

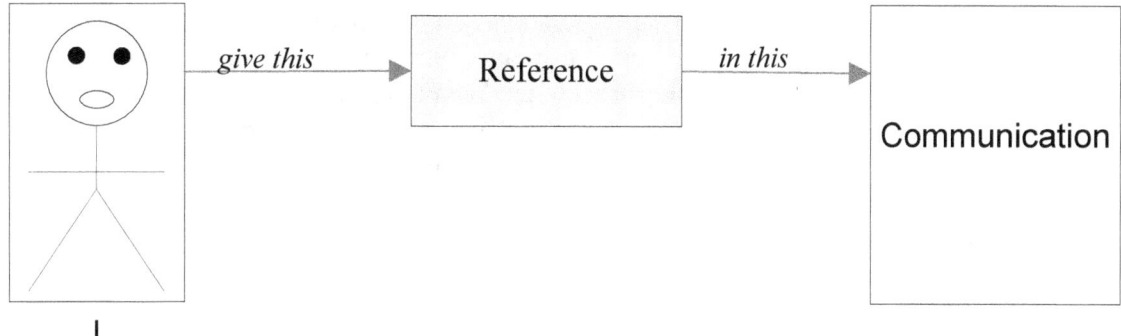

Since a reference contains principles, the origin of a reference is not important to us, but the reference itself is what is important to us. For this reason, the one who provides a reference to us is not important to know, but the reference itself is what is important for us to know. In this case, it is good to show that a reference is given without showing the one who provides that reference.

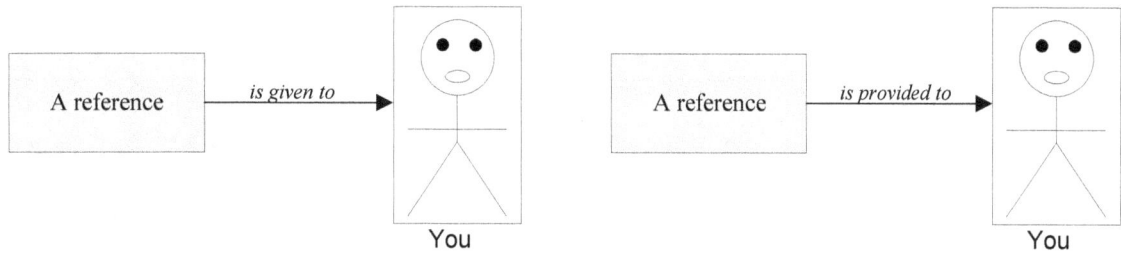

Since a reference is given in the form of communication and the one who provides the reference is not important to know, but the reference itself. In this case, it is possible for us to show that the reference is given in a communication without showing the one who provides that reference as shown by the diagram below.

Example Number 26

We use the continuity entity to show more entities that are not visible in the diagram. For instance, if our communication function includes many functions, it is possible for us to use the continuity entity to show more functions that are not listed in the diagram. Let's assume that our communication function is made of 6 functions as shown by the diagram below.

Communication Function

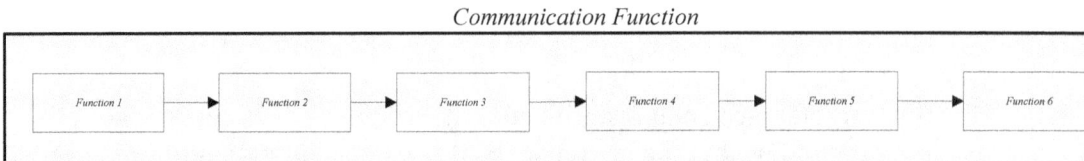

Since our communication function is made of several functions, while modeling our application, it may be possible for us not to show all the functions that include in our communication function. While the diagram above shows 6 functions, it is possible for us to use continuity to show some of those functions that are not in the diagram as shown below.

Communication Function

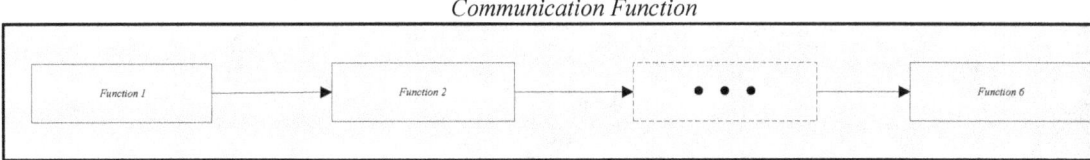

Example Number 27
The continuity entity can also be used to show list of entities in our application. For instance assume that we want to show at list of entities and some of those entities are not visible in the diagram, we can use the continuity entity to show that. Let's assume that within our application, we have a list of entities that is made of 6 entities as shown by this diagram.

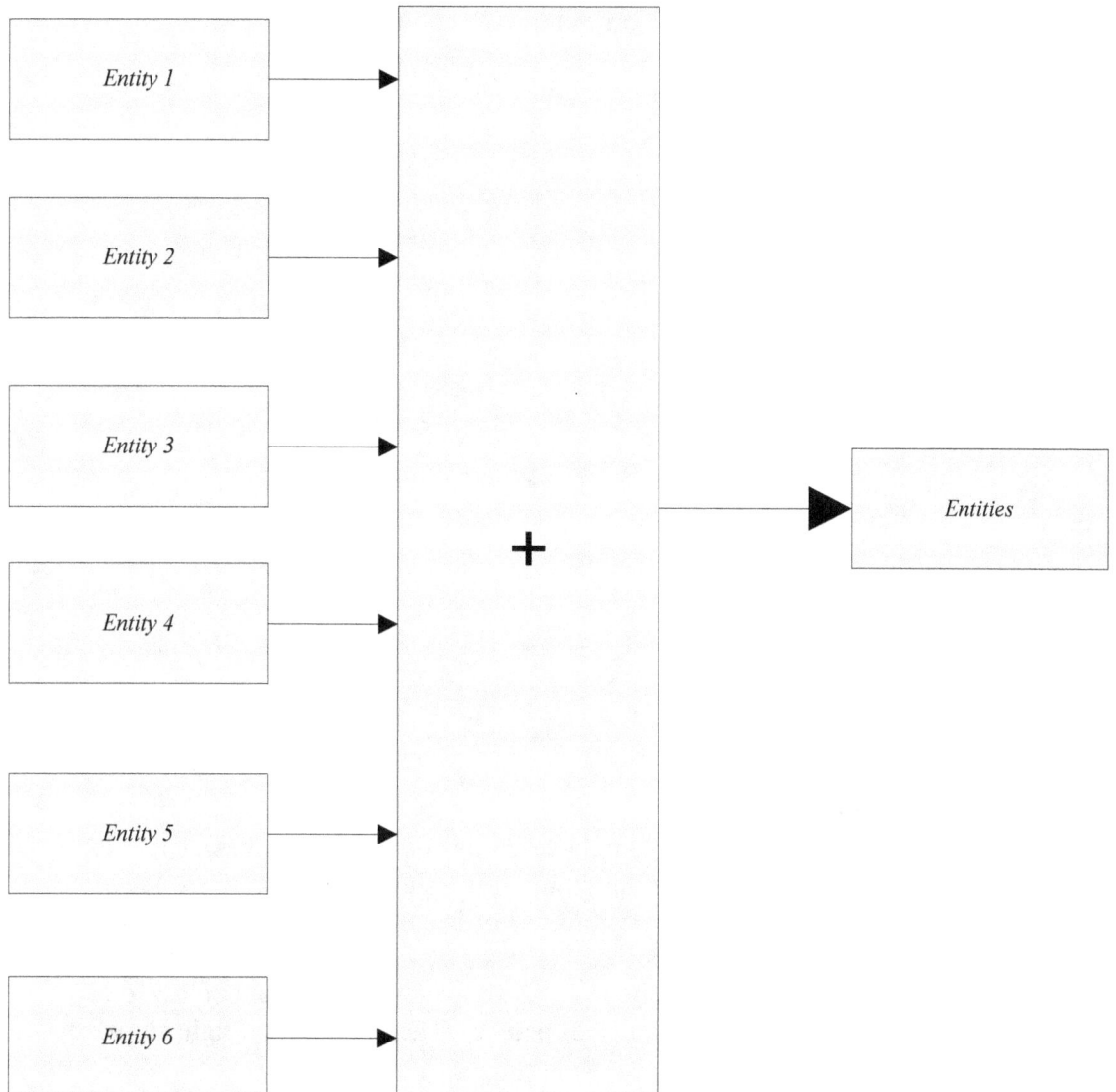

Let's assume that within our diagram it is not possible for us to show all the entities, and then we can use the continuity entity to show entities that are not visible as shown by this diagram. The usage of the continuity entity from the diagram above simply shows a list of entities that is not visible in the diagram. While we use the continuity entity before the last entity, we can also put the continuity at the end. Putting the continuity at the end shows that we don't know the end of the list.

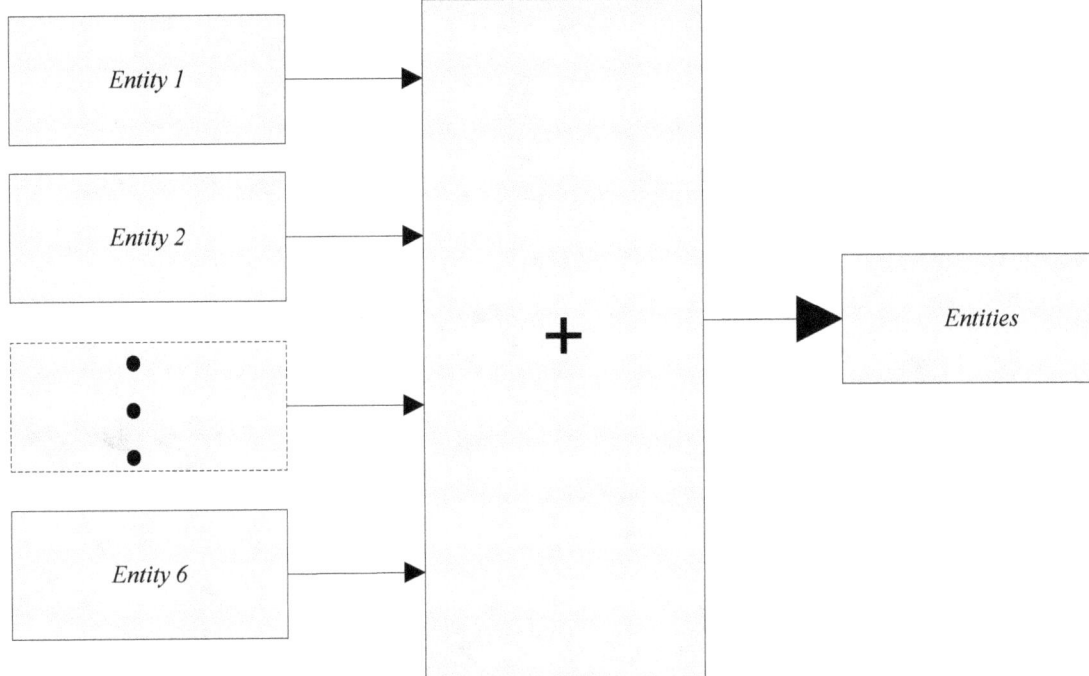

Example Number 27
In a project it is possible to have groups of people that have specific functions. We can use the group of people entity to show groups of people that make up our project. For instance assume that in a project, we have four groups of people. In this case, we can represent those groups of people by the diagram below. As shown by the diagram below, our project is made of 4 groups of people. The group to the right shows the total number of people in the project.

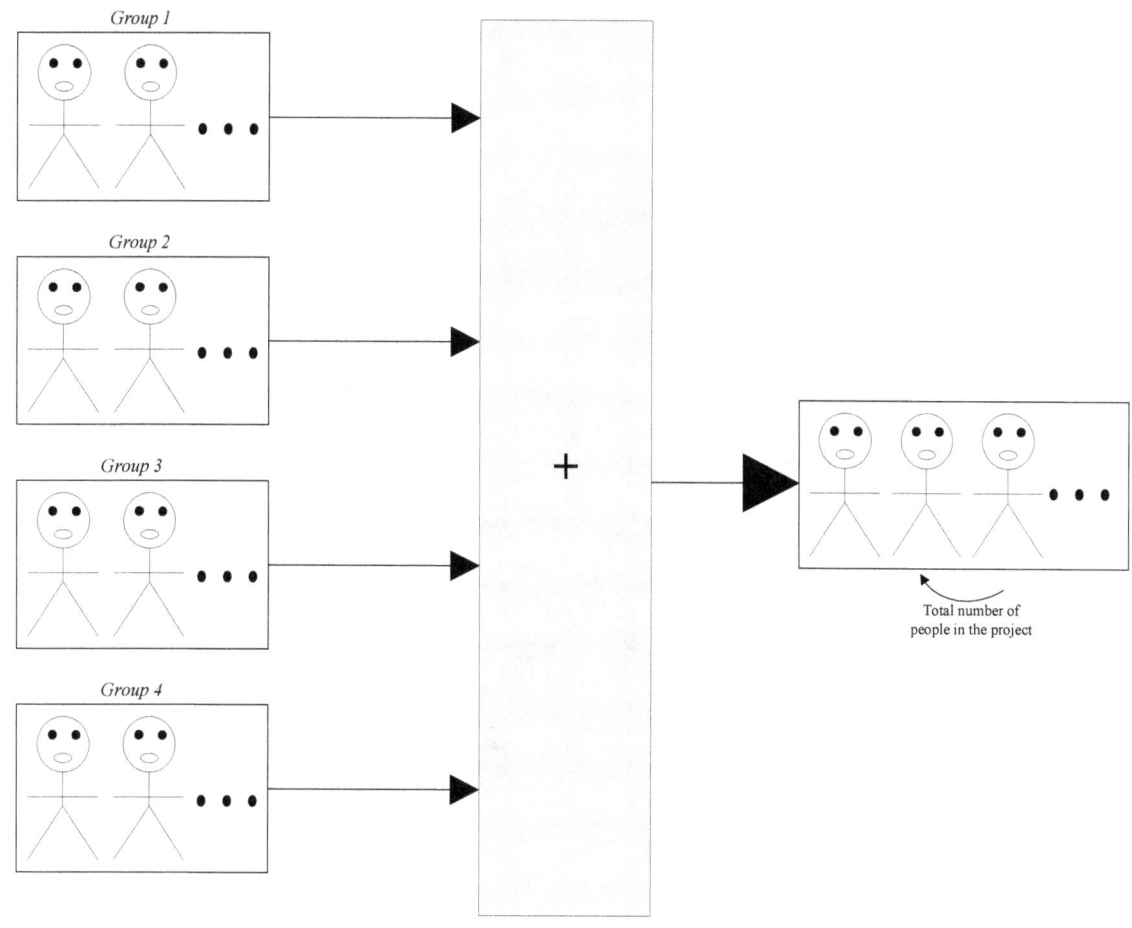

Total number of
people in the project

Example Number 28

Let's assume that we have a relationship diagram that shows the relationship between *entity 1, entity 2, entity 3,* and *entity* 4 as shown by the diagram below.

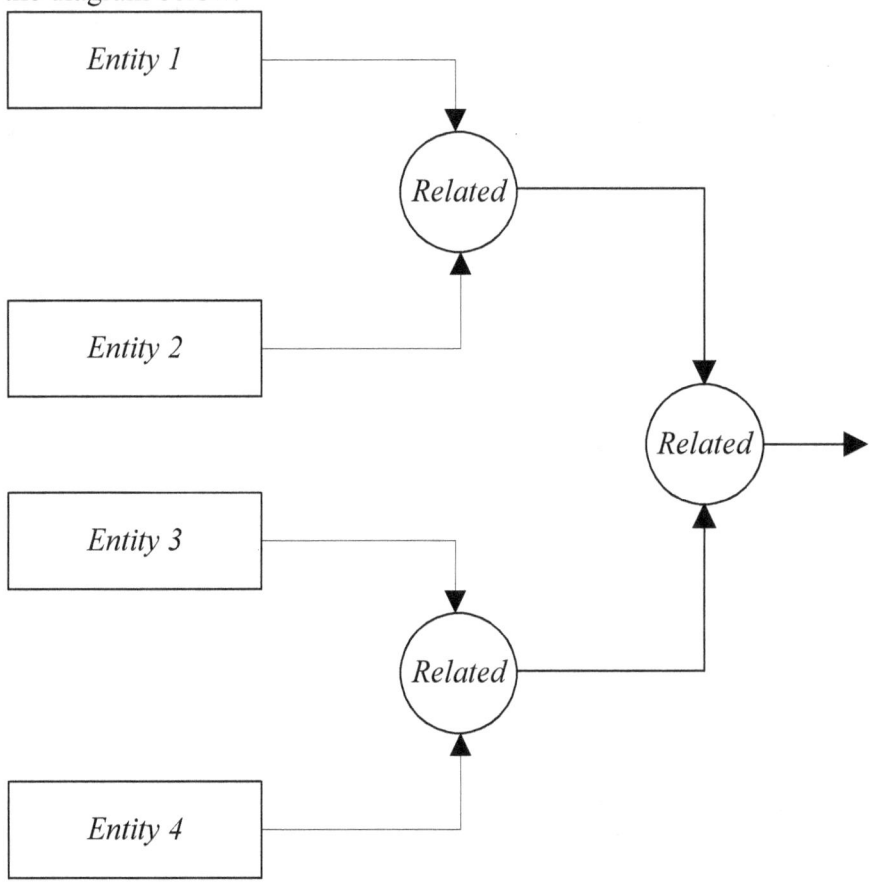

While we draw the relationship above to show multiple relationships or a relationship entity for 4 related entities; when having multiple entities in multiple relationships or multiple entities in a relationship, it is possible for us to define an entity at specific node. Since two entities are related by an entity, and that entity is considered to be the result of that relationship, it is possible for us to identify an entity at a node or identify it by a node as shown by the diagram below.

Let's assume that *entity 1* is related to *entity 2*, where that relationship is related to the relationship of *entity 3* related to *entity 4* as shown by the diagram above. To better understand the explanation, let's show that diagram above again with node number.

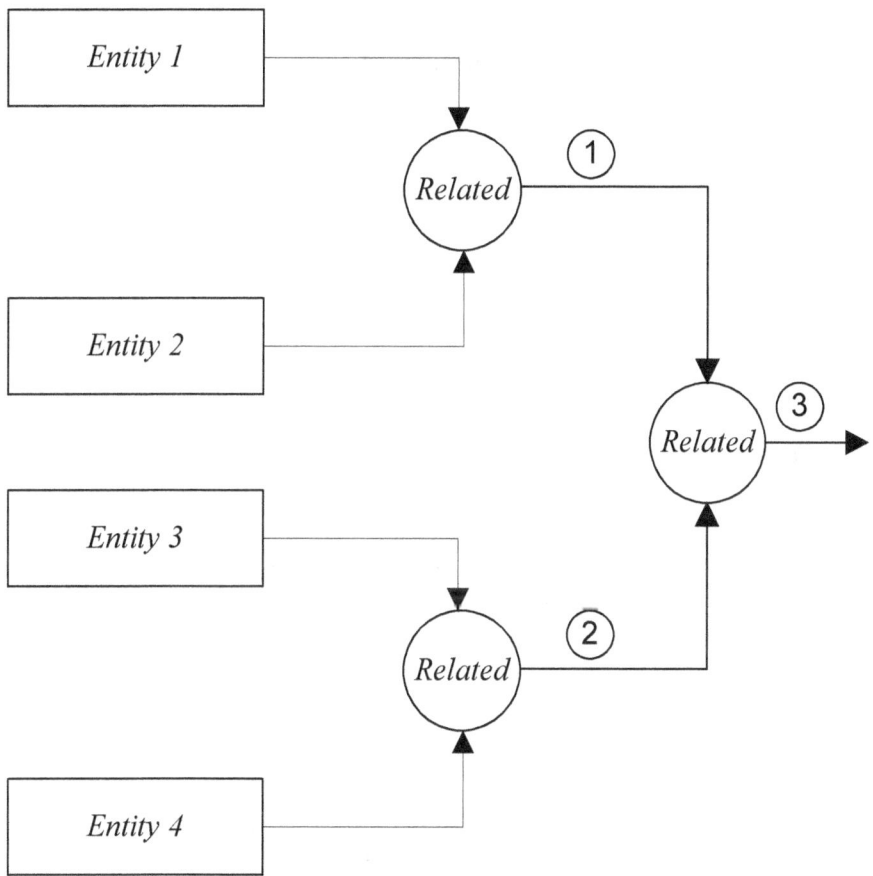

From the diagram above, we redraw the relationship again to show node number. In this case, we have node 1 that shows the relationship between *entity 1* and *entity 2,* node number 2 that shows the relationship of *entity* 3 and *entity* 4 and node 3 that shows the result of the relationship from node 1 and node 2. In this case, node 3 shows the relationship of the 2 relationships.

Now what we can do, we can identify entities for node 1, node 2, and node 3. Assume that we can identify the entity, entity 1 and entity 2 are related by, and then we can define that entity. Here, let's define or identify that entity as entity 5. Then we can identify the entity, entity 3 and entity 4 are related by entity 6, then we can identify the entity those two relationships are related as entity 7. What we have done here, we simply identify node 1 as entity 5, node 2 as entity 6, and node 3 as entity 7. In this case, we can redraw the relationship diagram in the form below with those entities.

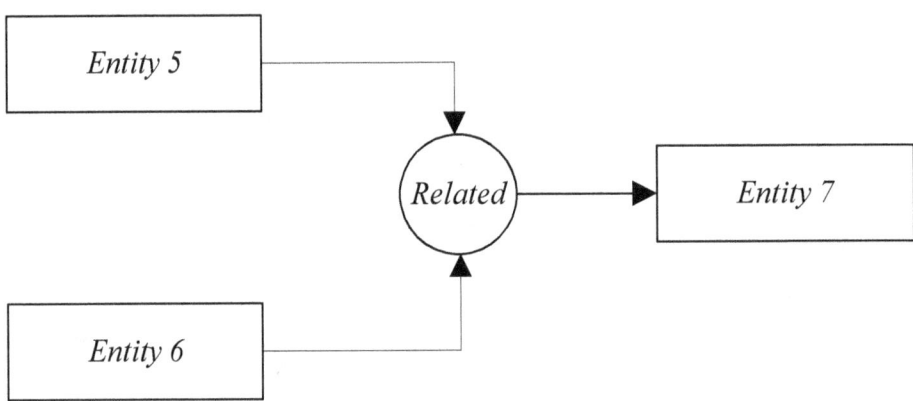

As we can see, if we can identify specific entity at specific node in a relationship, then we can reduce the number of entity in that relationship. Since there is no limit in a relationship in term of number, this process has no limit.

Example Number 29
Since it is more understandable for us to approach relationships one at a time, the separation line and the time line can be used together in a relationship diagram to show the way we approach or identify a relationship at a specific time. In other words, since it is better for us to

identify the relationship of two entities at a time, rather than several entities at a given time. In this case, we can use the separation line with time line to show how we approach or identify a relationship at a given time. For instance related to the diagram below, we identify relationship one which is the relationship of entity 1 and entity 2 and then later at time 2, we identity the result of that relationship in relationship with entity number 3 and so forth.

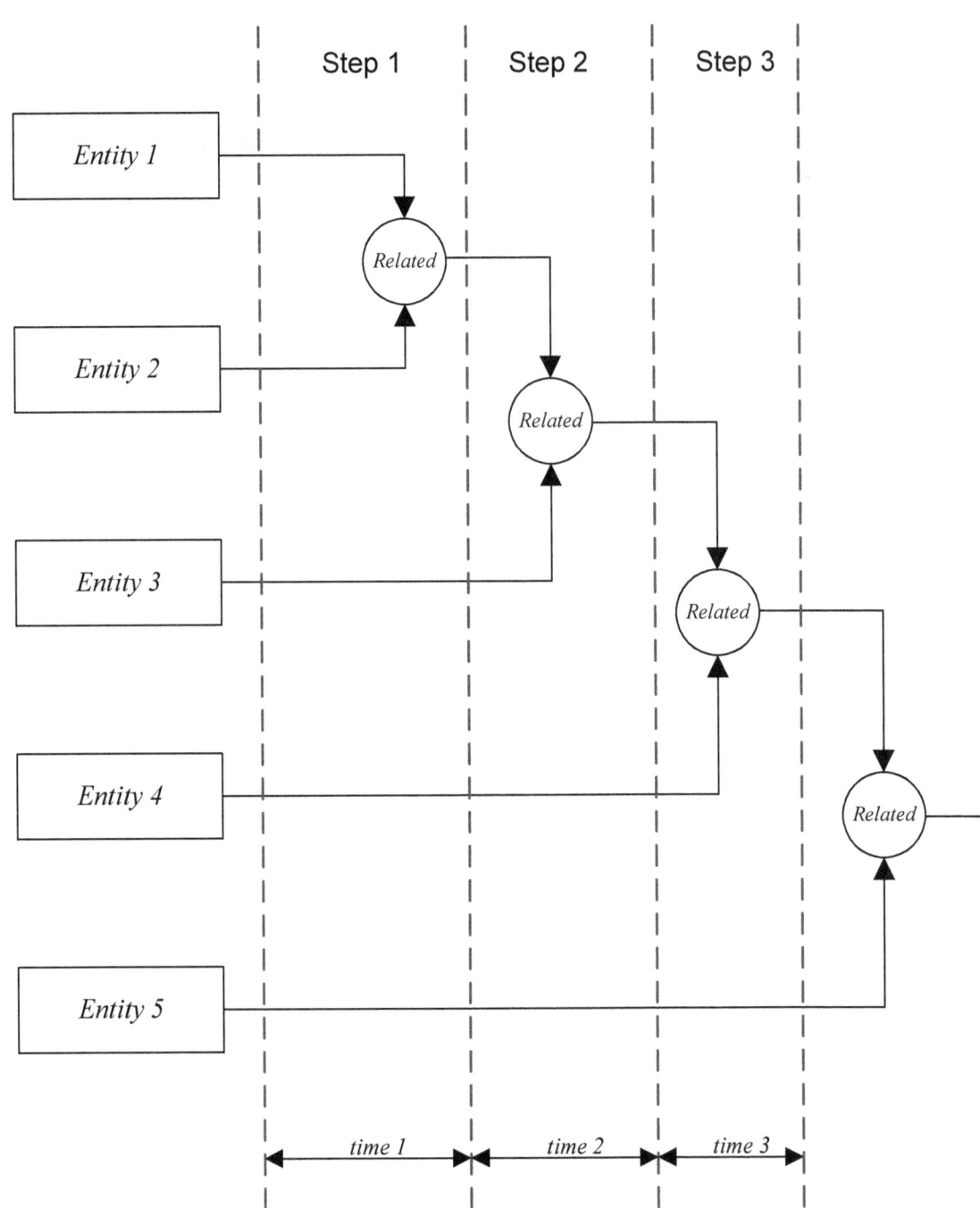

Example Number 30

Since our application depends on our understanding of the principle entity.
By having an operating principle, it is possible for us to follow that
principle in order for us to execute our project. Given that the application
itself depends on everybody in the project, it makes sense for those people
to follow the operating principle to enable the execution of the application.
Within the application itself, it makes sense for us to show everybody in
the application related to the principle of operation as shown by the
diagram below. The diagram below shows that we have six people in our
project. It does not matter in term of number of people we have, we can
still show them with the same operating principle. We can also use
continuity and group if space is an issue.

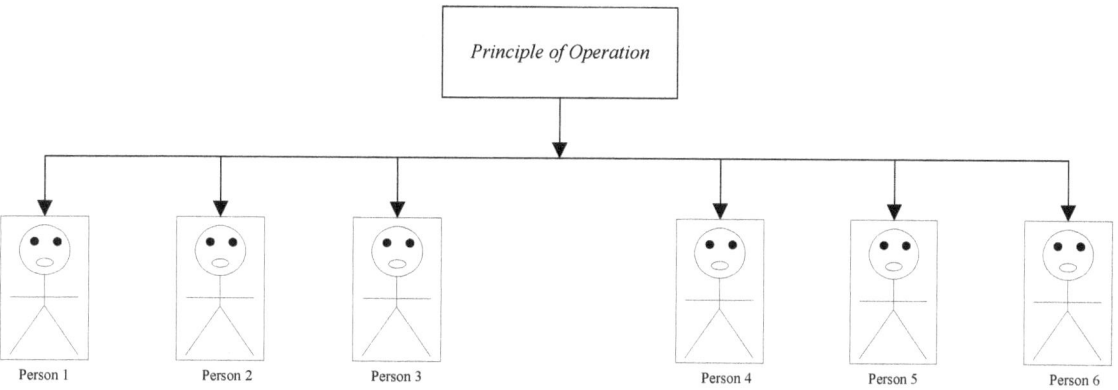

Example Number 31

Given that within the project itself, the status of a function is considered to
be an entity; similarity to the list of entity diagram, if necessary it may be
possible for us to show the status of each function that makes of our
application or the overall function as shown by the diagram below. In this
case, we can use the function name or the actual function and the
completion status of the function; for instance if our application or the
overall function of our application is made of 4 functions; then it is
possible for us to show the status diagram in the form below. The diagram
below shows the % completion of each function and the overall %
completion of the overall application.

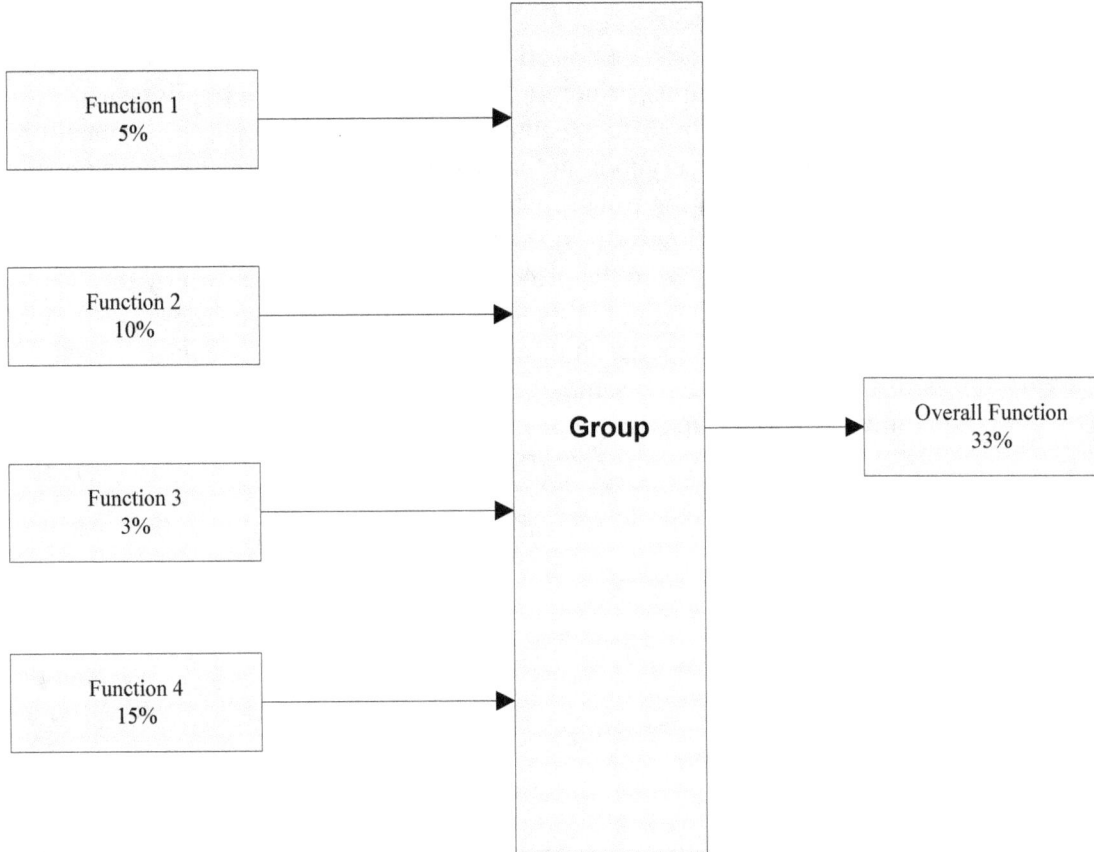

Example Number 32

The overall process of modeling enables us to model our application, disregard the type of that application. For instance, if our application is being viewed as a service that we provide, it is possible for us to model it. As well as, if our application is being viewed as a product that we develop, it is possible as well for us to model it in the same manner. In term of modeling our application, if the result of our application is being viewed as a service, that service is being viewed as an entity. As well as, if the result of our application is being viewed as a product that we make, that product is being viewed as an entity. By understanding that, if term of entity, it is possible for us to show or identify that entity within the model of our application. For instance, if our application is to produce a physical entity, then we can show that entity produced by our project or our application in the form below. We can call it any name or its actual name, here we simply call it *Entity One*.

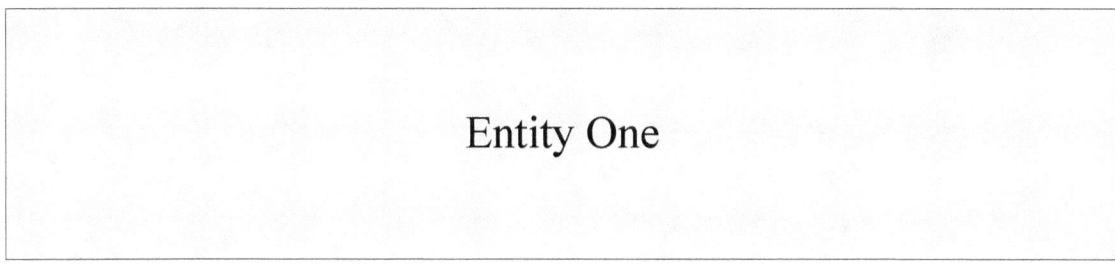

From the diagram above, *Entity One* is being viewed as the entity produced by our application or our project. If the purpose of our project is to provide a service or service an entity, then *Entity One* is being viewed as well as the service we provide. Since an entity must have a function and the function of an entity is also an entity, then it is possible for us to show *Entity One* and its function in the form below. Here we use the name *Function 1* as the name of the function of the entity; we can use any name we want or the actual name of that function.

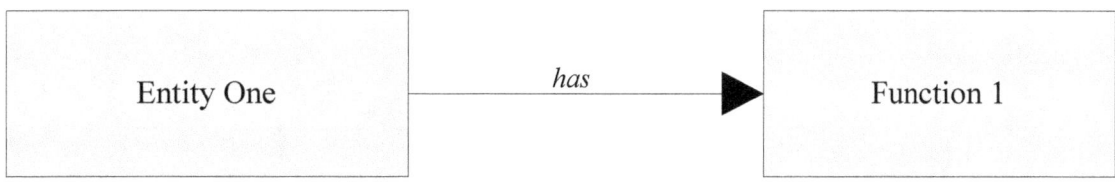

The diagrams above show the entity produced by our application and the function of that entity. Given that an entity can have several parts and each part of an entity can be a function, within our application, it may be possible as well to extend the diagrams above to the form below. From the diagrams below, the first one to the left shows a list of entity or list of part of entity produced by our application, while the one to the right shows the function of each entity or each part of the entity.

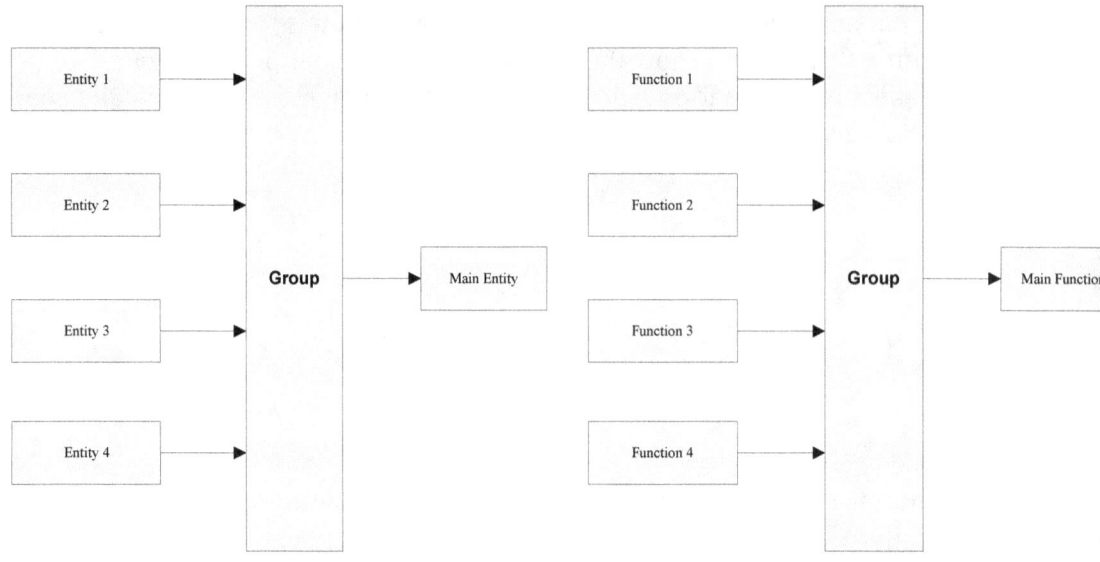

From the diagrams above, the main entity is being viewed as the entity produced by our application. While in the second diagram, the main function is being viewed as the function of the main entity. Sine the main entity is made of several parts, if we wan to, we can show it as a group of entity or a group of parts of entity, and so does the main function. While we show both diagrams in the form above, we can also show them in the other form below.

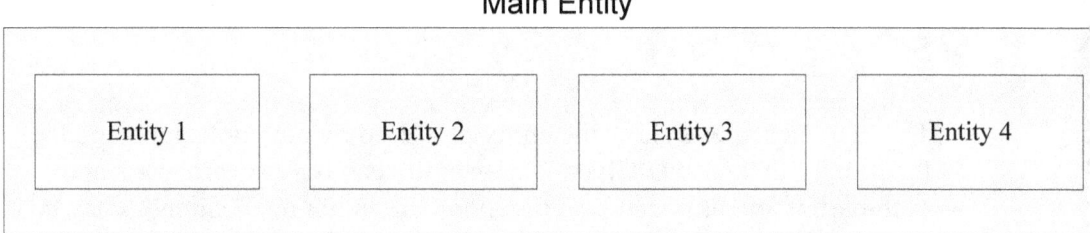

Main Function

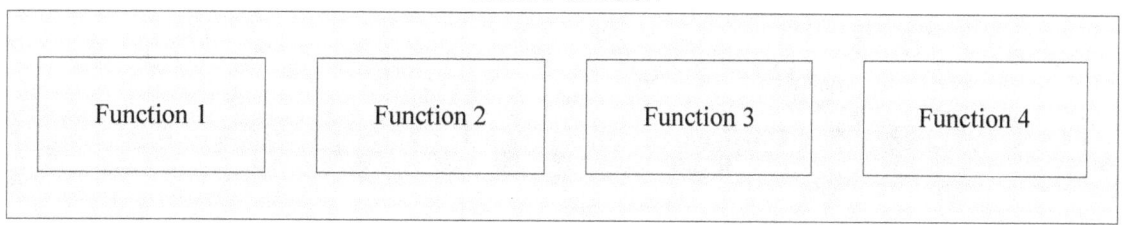

Related to the diagram above, since entities that we use in our application must have functions, in this case we can use several entities in our application to execute a function. The way to look at it, several entities in our application can have one or more function. Assume that *Entity 1*, *Entity 2*, and *Entity 3* in our application have *Function 2*. In this case, we can show that by the diagram below.

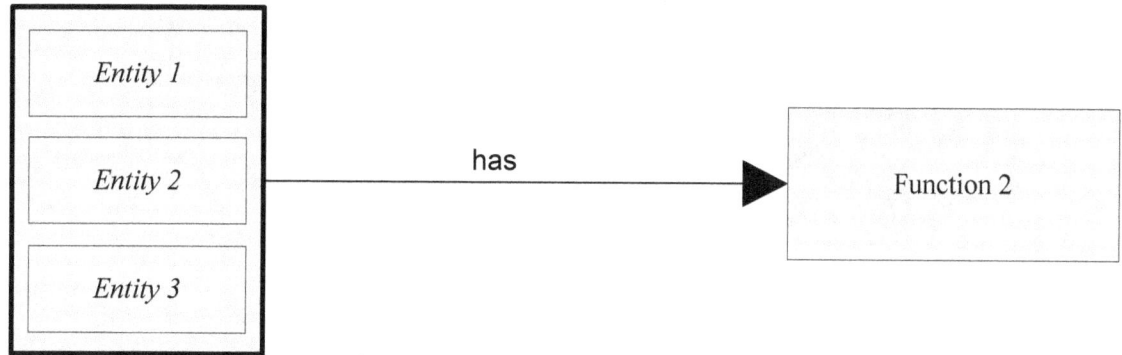

Example Number 33
In an application or project, it may be required for us to use many entities in order or us to execute the function of that application. Within the project itself, if we use entities or external entities to help us execute our function, it makes sense for us to show the list of entities that we use in the project. The diagram below shows a list of entities that we use to help us execute the function of our application.

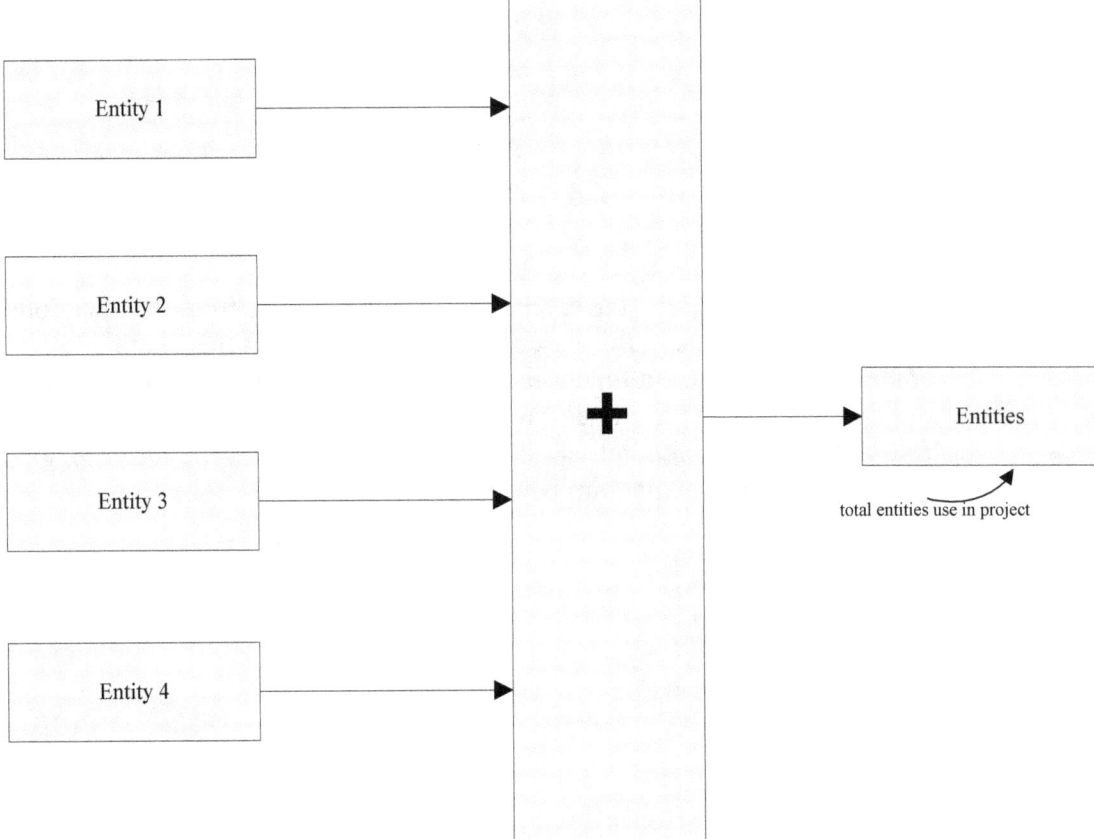

While we use the diagram above to show the list of entities we use in our project, we don't have to show it in that form. We can also show in any other form.

Example Number 34
From the above example, we have shown the list of entities that are used in our application. In this case, we show the list of entities that we use to enable us to execute the function of our application. Since we use those entities to help us execute our project, it makes sense for us to show that in a diagram, where we can show that the people in the application actually use those entities to execute the application. By doing so, we can show that in the form presented below. In the first diagram, we show that

Person 1 in the application uses *Entity 1* to execute *Function 1*. In this case, *Function 1* is considered to be the function of *Person 1* in the application.

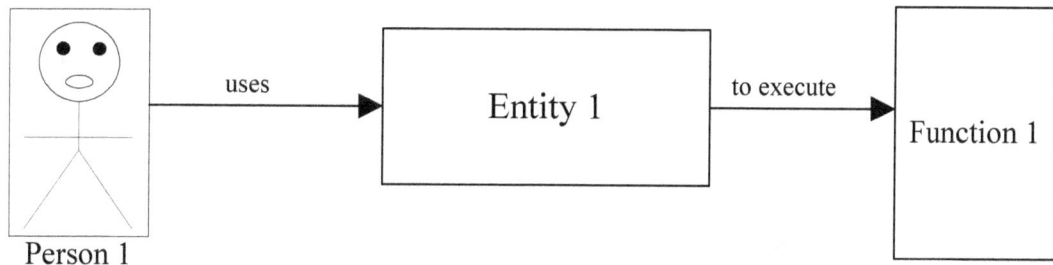

If our application has more than one person, in this case our application has many people. It makes sense to show the entities they use to execute the application. By doing so, we can say that a group of people use a group of entities to execute the application or the function of the application. In this case, we have the diagram below. The function to the right is considered to be the function of our application.

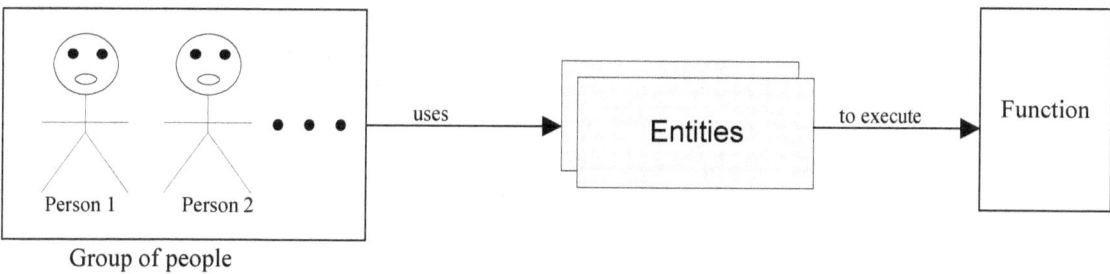

Example Number 35

By understanding the example above, we can see that the principle entity or the analysis entity can be used to show the analysis of an entity that we use to execute a function. Assume that we are working in a project where we use an entity to execute a function, in this case we can use the analysis entity in conjunction with that entity to show that analysis of that entity as shown by the diagram below.

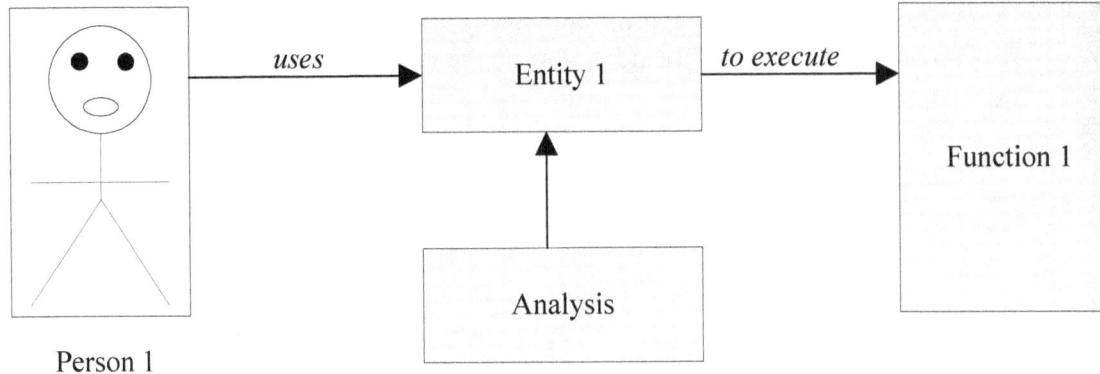

Person 1

From the diagram above, we can see that *Entity 1* which is used by *Person 1* to execute *Function 1* is under analysis. From the same diagram, *Function 1* may well be the function of *Entity 1*, so it makes sense to analyze *Entity 1* related to *Function 1* in that application.

Example Number 36
To better understand the usage of the location entity, let's assume that our application includes many people, where those people operate at separate locations while working together to execute the functions of our application. In this case, in each location, people who work in that application have their own functions in terms of groups. To better understand that, let's assume we have 4 groups of people where they work at separate locations. Below the main function of the application is related to the functions of the groups in the form of

Main Function

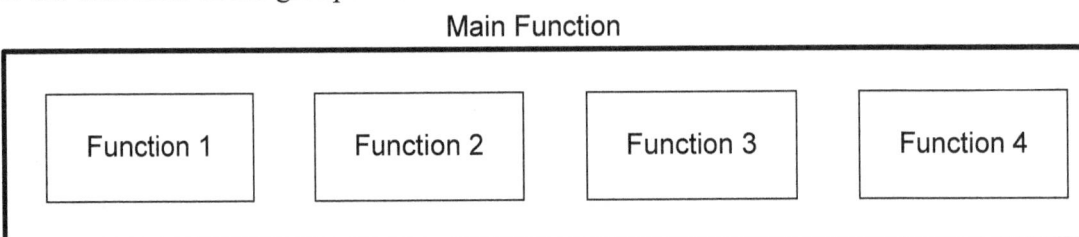

From the diagram above, the main function is considered the overall function of our application, where *Function 1* is considered the function of *Group 1*; *Function 2* is considered the function of *Group 2* etc. Here the overall function of the main application is made of 5 functions, where each function is considered to be part of the application function. In this case if we want to, it is possible for us to show the locations or the sites of operation of those groups of people in the form below.

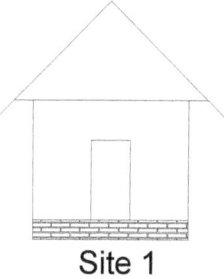

Site 1

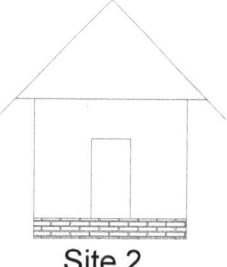

Site 2

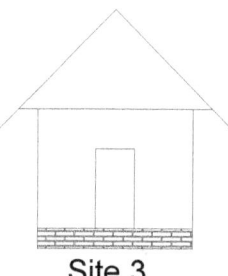

Site 3

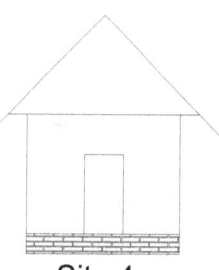

Site 4

Since the people in the sites or at the locations communicate together to execute the function of the application, if we want to we can show the connection of the sites in the form shown below.

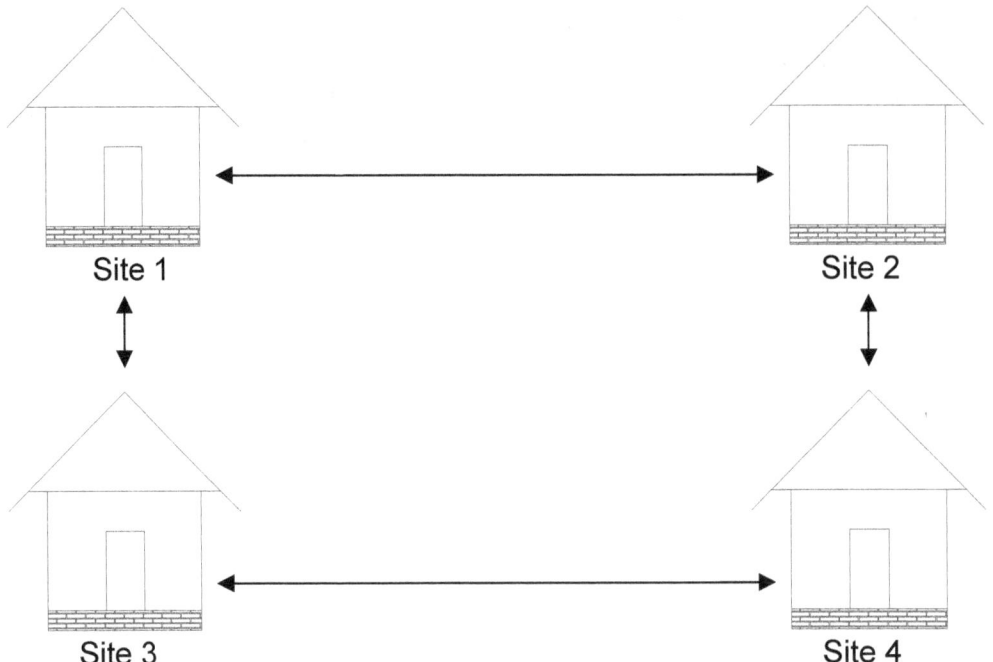

Example Number 37

By understanding our parent principle, it is possible for us to operate at multiple locations. Since our application should not take location into consideration, our understanding of the principle enables us to operate at multiple places, where we do not take specific place into consideration. Let's assume that we operate in 4 areas, then we can use the area entity to show the places that we operate as shown by the diagram below.

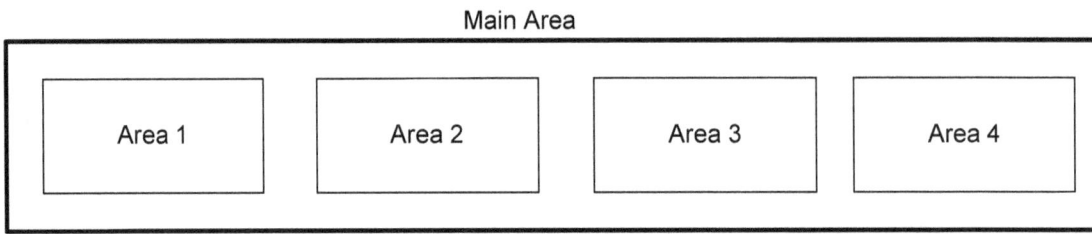

The areas that we operate can be viewed as entities; they can also be viewed as countries as well. We can use the area entity to show that we operate in multiple countries or cities. If we want to, we can use the main area entity to show the cities or the countries that we operate in the form below. The usage of the form below assumes that we understand our parent principles and that makes is possible for us to operate in multiple countries. In this case we can show those countries in this form

Main Area

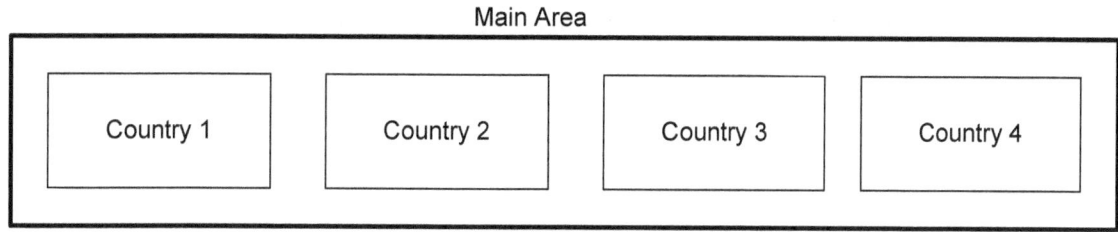

Since our understanding of our parent principles does not limit our mobility, with that understanding, it is possible for us to extend our services to other locations where problems are identified and need to be solved by our services. In this case, related to the diagram above, we can show the sketches of the actual countries we are operating in the form below.

Main Area

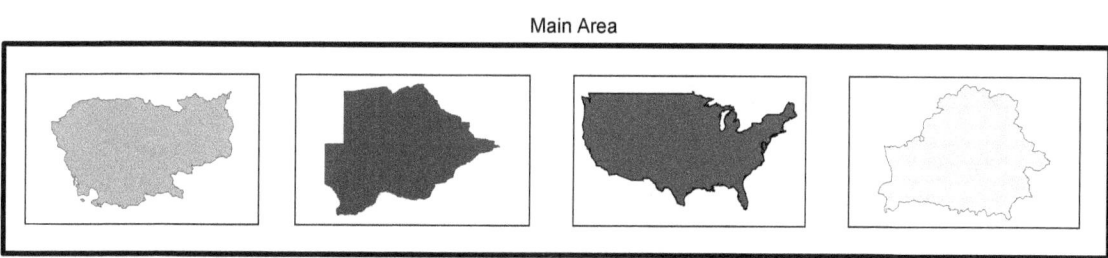

Error Identification and Correction Charts

In order for the error to be corrected, it must be identified; in order for the error to be identified, the communication or the process must be analyzed. We can use the error identification and correction charts listed below to identify errors in our communications.

Error Identification

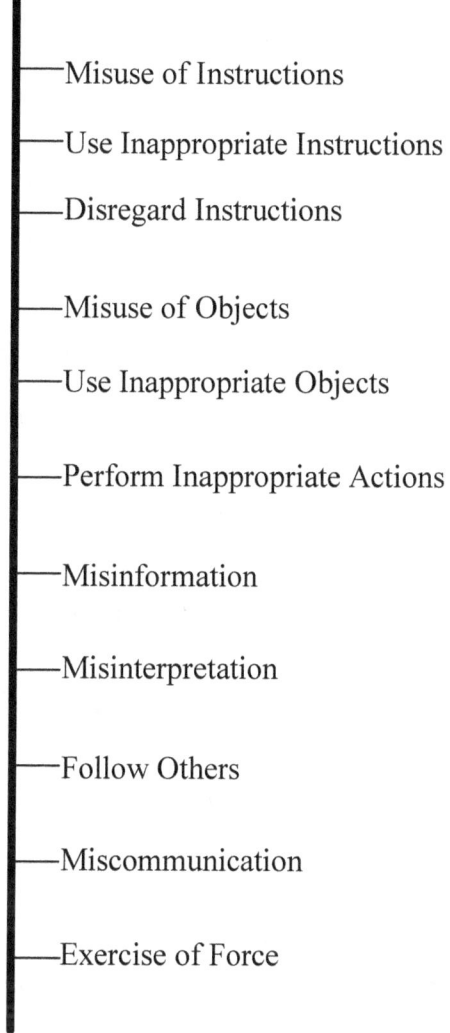

—Misuse of Instructions

—Use Inappropriate Instructions

—Disregard Instructions

—Misuse of Objects

—Use Inappropriate Objects

—Perform Inappropriate Actions

—Misinformation

—Misinterpretation

—Follow Others

—Miscommunication

—Exercise of Force

Error Correction

- Good Usage of Instructions
- Use Appropriate Instructions
- Regard Instructions

- Good Usage of Objects
- Use Appropriate Objects

- Perform Appropriate Actions

- Proper Information

- Good Interpretation

- Follow Principles

- Proper Communication

- Exercise of Kindness

Error in Sentence

- Use of Bad Words

- Use of Bad Expressions

- Use of Non Portable Words

- Use of Non Portable Expressions

- Use of Words with Multiple Meanings

Correction Consideration

—Use of Good Words

—Use of Good Expressions

—Use of Portable Words

—Use of Portable Expressions

—Use of Words with Single Meaning

Conclusion

It is very important for us to model our application and understand the process of modeling our project in the communication domain. Since communication enables us to do what we do, and we depend on communication to do our work, it is very important to use communication to model what we do. It is also important not to take communication for granted within what we do.

When we model our project in the communication domain, we look at what we do from the flow of our communication. In this case, we can detect and correct errors in a costless manner before they happen. Now that we finish our project and verify that everything is working accordingly, we can then present it or deliver it to our customers. Since communication is not limited by us, since we are not limited by our communication, after delivering or presenting the project to our customers, they may still have questions for us that we need to answer. Now that we understand the process of modeling our project in the communication domain, we should not limit ourselves from communication.

From the paragraph above, we have learned that we are not limited to communication and our customer can question us about the project after being delivered or presented. Now assume that our customers have provided us with two hundred hours to complete the project. We use the time to complete the project and we deliver it to the customers. Upon delivering the project to the customers, they are very happy with what we have done. In addition to that, they told us they will provide us with additional time, so we can tell them how we have completed the project. The question here is how we did what we have done. From what we have said, it is certain that we still have questions to answer to our customers.

.

Exercises

For some of us who may have questions about the warning messages, the following exercise can be used as a verification of our understanding of the principle. By having a good understanding of the principle, there should be no problem or ambiguity to verify the warning messages. Also, people who have a good understanding of the principle and who have worked out various exercise from the beginning to the end of the book, should have no problem with the error messages. The understanding of those error messages can be used as a verification to determine whether or not the principle of communication is understood. For some of us who have some difficulty to understand those error messages, turn them off and start working some exercises from the beginning to the end of the principle of communication book.

Since any entity can be used according to us and what we are doing, the exercises are not in order in terms of weights. We can do whatever we think we understand and leave the rest for later. As we make progress learning and understanding the principle, then we can move to do the ones we have left out. While the exercises are given here, they should not be the starting point of learning the principle. To understand the warning messages, it is better to start learning the principle from the understanding the principle of communication book or with the help of an instructor.

1. Show that a person cannot be deleted or erased

2. Verify that a person cannot be copied

3. Show that a person cannot be composed

4. Show that a person cannot be decomposed

5. Verify that a person cannot be grouped with other entity

6. Verify that a person cannot be rotated or flipped

7. Determine that it is not possible to compose a group of people

8. Show that a word cannot be deleted

9. Show that a word cannot be copied

10. Determine that a word cannot be composed and decomposed

11. Verify that an entity cannot be rotated or flipped. You may need to look at the aspect of the entity itself related to rotation. You may also need to look the function of the entity related to rotation as well.

12. Determine that an entity cannot be composed or decompose

13. Show that the function of our communication cannot be deleted

14. Show that the function of our communication cannot be copied

15. Verify that the function of our communication cannot be composed

16. Verify that an application cannot be deleted

17. Show that an application cannot be copied

18. Determine that the result of an application cannot be deleted

19. Show that the result of an application cannot be copied

20. Show that our communication cannot be composed

21. Verify that the communication function cannot be composed

22. Show that the result of our communication can not be composed and decomposed

23. Verify that it is not possible to copy and delete a timeline

24. Show that it is not possible to compose and decompose a timeline

25. Show that the progress of our application cannot be deleted or copied

26. Verify that the progress of our application cannot be composed and decomposed

27. Show that a node or a callout cannot be deleted or copied

28. Verify that a node and a callout cannot be composed and decomposed

29. Verify that an error cannot be deleted

30. Determine whether or not a problem can be deleted

31. Show that principles cannot be deleted

32. Verify that a compensator cannot be deleted or erased

33. Show that a compensator cannot be copied

34. Show that principles cannot be copied

35. Show that principles cannot be composed and decomposed

36. Determine that the Error Correction Function cannot be deleted or erased

37. Show that the Error Correction Function cannot be copied

38. Verify that the Error Correction Function cannot be composed and decomposed

39. Verify that an action cannot be deleted

40. Determine that an action cannot be copied

41. Verify that a reason cannot be deleted

42. Show that a reason cannot be copied

43. Show that a reason cannot be composed and decomposed

44. Verify with a practical example that a communication holder cannot be deleted and copied

45. Show that a sentence cannot be deleted and copied

46. Show that communication cannot be deleted and copied

47. Verify that information cannot be deleted

48. Show that it is not possible to copy information

49. Show that it is not possible to compose information

50. Determine that information cannot be decomposed

51. Determine the relationship between the word entity, the sentence entity, and the paragraph entity

52. Verify that a word and a sentence cannot be rotated

53. Determine that a reference cannot be deleted.

54. Show that a reference cannot be compose

55. Verify that a reference cannot be decompose

56. What is the difference between a written word and the word itself? Written word means a word on paper, board, postcard, etc.

57. Verify that information cannot be edited. If you want to, you may provide a practical example.

58. Determine the difference between a single entity and a group of entity

59. Show that a reference cannot be edited

60. Show that a reference cannot be copied

61. Verify that the relationship entity cannot be deleted

62. Sow that the relationship entity cannot be rotated

63. Determine that the relationship entity cannot be copied

64. Verify whether or not it is possible to combine people with communication function.

65. Determine whether or not it is possible to group people with application. This is the same as saying that, determine whether or not it is possible to group the people with the application entity.

66. Show that question cannot be deleted

67. Verify that a question cannot be copied

68. Show that a question cannot be composed and decomposed

69. Verify that a question cannot be rotated

70. Show that the answer of a question cannot be deleted

71. Verify that the answer of a question cannot be copied

72. Show that the answer of a question cannot be composed and decomposed

73. Verify that the answer of a question cannot be rotated

74. Verify that the answer of a question cannot be edited

75. Show that a question cannot be edited

76. Verify that the match label cannot be deleted

77. Show that the mach label cannot be copied

78. Verify that the point to label cannot be rotated

79. Show that the point to label cannot be copied

80. Show that the agreement label cannot be deleted

81. Verify that the agreement label cannot be copied

82. Show that the inclusion label cannot be deleted

83. Verify that the inclusion label cannot be copied

84. Verify that the relationship between two entities cannot be deleted

85. Show that the relationship between two entities cannot be copied

86. Verify that the relationship between two entities cannot be edited

87. Verify that an entity cannot be composed. In this case, you verify your understanding about building or deriving an entity.
88. What does a project identification mean to you? In this case you verify your understanding about a project identification.

www.ingramcontent.com/pod-product-compliance
Lightning Source LLC
Chambersburg PA
CBHW081443170526
45166CB00008B/2295